# A SHIFT TO BLISS

THE SEVEN BELIEFS

THAT LIMIT LOVE, HAPPINESS, PEACE AND PROSPERITY …

*SET YOURSELF FREE!*

Nicole Bayliss

***A Shift to Bliss***



Published by Nicole Bayliss, first published in 2017
Email: info@nicolebayliss.com.au
http://nicolebayliss.com.au

Cover design by Marie Svenungsson Schyberg,
Swedesign, http://swedesignstudio.com.au

Printed by Lightning Source

Bayliss, Nicole

ISBN 978-0-9875138-2-3

# CONTENTS

"There's a crack, a crack in everything.

That's how the light gets in."

– Leonard Cohen

# INTRODUCTION

***This is a book of light. Its purpose is to bring awareness to the hidden beliefs that may be sabotaging your life, and to shine the light of truth so that you may know true happiness and fulfilment. Many of us believe that our lives create our beliefs, but really, our beliefs create our lives. What if I told you that your parents told you lies? They didn't intend to. Their parents told them lies too, and theirs before them, and back it went, through the generations, one lie building upon another, each generation believing them, and living lives created out of them. It wasn't their fault that they believed in the lies, and it's not yours, because they so easily disguise themselves as the truth …***

## Let's begin with the truth

You are not the person who struggles through life, who doesn't have enough time, money, peace or love. You are not the "you" who worries about the future or the "you" who ruminates on the past. That is the little "you" who belongs to the story of your life so far. And while every story is important and has meaning, we must remember that it is only a story. It is not necessarily the truth. The True You exists beyond the story, because your story has been created from everything that the little you believes. These beliefs were given to you from your family and society and further created from your life experiences to date. Beyond the story of your life, you are a being of infinite potential and your natural and authentic state is bliss. You are here to discover that limitless potential and to live it. You are here to go beyond what you have been conditioned to believe and you have all the resources within you to create Heaven on Earth. Beyond the drama of life sits within us a well of bliss, and from this place – and only this place - we can move beyond our current reality and create the life we truly want.

Many of our conditioned beliefs cause inner and outer turmoil, but beliefs that align with the Universal Truth bring a shift to bliss. There are no accidents. This book is in your hands for a reason. Now is the time to bring conscious awareness to the lies you believe – the negative fear-based beliefs that keep you trapped. Every sad story, every disappointment, problem and block to moving forward, when distilled down to its root cause, was created from a belief that doesn't serve you. Maybe you already know or suspect this, or recognise a glimmer of the truth. The truth is not the one we have been conditioned to believe, but a reality without limitations and of infinite potential.

I am not asking you to believe what I am saying, but perhaps create a space to become open to the idea that our reality is created entirely by us. For many, life is a struggle. At times it can feel like a journey of disappointment, heartache and hopelessness, with happiness a fleeting state of being. To varying degrees, most of us believe in a limited world and our own limited presence and potential within it. We haven't yet woken up to knowing that every experience, whether we see it as positive or negative, is here to show us something about what we believe.

## What this book is not

This is not a book about "positive thinking". Life is a rich tapestry – it can be exciting, bland, devastating, sad and joyful. It contains everything! Many of us are addicted to the idea that we are supposed to feel positive most of the time and that if we don't, there is something wrong with us. This is not the truth. If we want to live full and meaningful lives, we must feel our full range of emotions. This is a book about transformation and genuinely shifting our subconscious core beliefs, which we may not be aware of, to the truth of who we really are. It will bring awareness to your "blind spots", and enable you to see your life through a different lens, empowering you to make choices that lead to a fulfilling and authentic life.

## How to use this book

You can read this book from start to finish, or you can go to the Contents page and choose to read just the chapters that resonate with you. At the end of each chapter are affirmations to assist you in releasing your old belief and align you to the truth. Affirmations are powerful, because whatever we tell ourselves is absorbed by the subconscious mind, which then goes about creating our new reality. On page 14 I suggest some different ways to become more present and self-aware, and on page 19 I suggest a daily meditation technique. These are not a prerequisite for releasing the seven beliefs, but will enhance your experience of this book and bring greater awareness into your life.

## A little about me

My human story is like so many – childhood wounds, marriage, children, divorce, happy times and sad times. My spiritual journey began many years ago through experiencing, studying and practicing healing therapies. Through meditation, I learned to become present and to listen to Source, and gain awareness of the power of the human mind. The mind is our computer. If it is programmed correctly, it serves us well, but if the programming is faulty or a virus enters the computer, it affects everything created from that computer. Whatever the mind believes, it creates. My healing and coaching work has this concept at its core – "change your mind, and you change your life".

There are many and varied beliefs, but beneath these many beliefs are common themes, and each of these themes is an umbrella for the rest. I now present these to you in this book. As with any project that is undertaken with love and inspiration, much of this work is not from me. It has come to you via me, from the Source. I am no guru. Most of the time I am present and aware and blissful, but like most of us on the journey to awakening, awareness can fly out the window if I am challenged, stressed or tired. I am faced with certain life challenges, like everybody else on this planet. Occasionally I struggle to find a sense of inner peace. I do however, know that I have the power and the resources within me to access an inner state of bliss even in the most challenging of times, because a shift to bliss is not dependent upon circumstances. A shift to bliss is an inner state that we can achieve through awareness and changing our mind.

I am a flawed human being who has struggled with her own self-worth, made mistakes and lacked trust in the process of life, and yet I am also a seeker of the truth. Like many before me, the pain in my life has propelled me to seek answers. My hope is that this book may help you find answers to your life challenges, and that you may grow in awareness, love, peace and joy.

**Whatever you believe you create**

What you believe has created your life to date. Perhaps you believe that your life has been created partly from your own choices and partly from outside influences over which you have no control? From our limited ego mind perspective this is true, but as already mentioned, you are not just the little human you. You are far greater than you can imagine – you are an energy field whose beliefs, thoughts and feelings are constantly creating. Most of us are unaware of just how powerful our ability to create is. So much of what we create happens at the subconscious level – a level that is inaccessible to most of us - and so the little you sees situations and events as separate and uncontrollable. Everything that happens to you is a reflection of a belief in a truth or a lie which created the circumstance. When we are aligned with the truth, we create fulfilling outcomes, and when we are aligned with a lie, our lives feel difficult and ultimately unfulfilling. When we hold a self-limiting belief, our mind focuses on evidence that supports it. Messages to the contrary will be ignored or dismissed.

## Why would we create negative events in our life?

Many of us have experienced extraordinarily painful events or know of people who have experienced something they didn't deserve. We see so much suffering in the world and at the human ego level we find it hard to accept that every being is creating their own reality, when the realities being created by many are not what anyone would consciously choose. And they were not consciously chosen! All unfavourable circumstances are created by us so as to become conscious and to grow. Some were created by the ego mind (the little you) and this is also known as karma. Karma is simply the

Universal law of "you reap what you sow". For many of us it can be difficult to realise the connection between the initial source of an event and the subsequent creation of it, because there is a time lag between the sowing of the seed and its sprouting. The truth is that we don't get away with anything. If we say or do something that hurts someone else, the Universe will re-balance this, even if it takes years to do so. We also create unfavourable situations and events at the soul level, also known as a soul contract. Our soul chooses this experience for our growth and evolution. Many of us use up a lot of energy thinking "Why me? This is so unfair. I really don't deserve this", and yet at the soul level we created it. Soul contract challenges test the human spirit to transform at a deep level. When bad things happen, it is a normal human reaction to feel victimised, angry or even to seek revenge. The ego mind is challenged like never before. The event or circumstance is a vehicle to our awakening. The pain pushes us to awaken and see things differently, because awakening is the only way we will be able to transcend the pain.

## Now is the time to become aware of our beliefs

Everything we believe creates energy, and from this energy our lives manifest. Discovering and letting go of a self-limiting belief or "lie" is like throwing off a heavy backpack we have been burdened with all our lives. We thought that the contents of the backpack were necessary, until we realised they weren't. When we drop the pack, we discover, for the first time, we can feel lighter and freer.

Just as once upon a time the human race believed that the Earth was flat and the stars in the heavens revolved solely around the Earth, a new truth was revealed which changed our perspective and we now know that the Earth is but a small planet in the midst of an expanding Universe. The more aware we are that not everything is the truth, the more willing we will be to examine the lies we believe and to let them go, allowing us to know true freedom.

## The ripple effect

Just as our outer lives reflect our inner lives, the state of the world reflects the mass consciousness of the earth's inhabitants. Most of us would agree that there is a polarisation in our world right now of "good" and "evil" that is becoming ever more intense. While many people are experiencing a profound spiritual awakening, another part of the earth's population is sick, existing in a vibration of fear and hatred, created from a collective of fearful ego minds. This polarisation or "split" is a reflection of what is present in most minds. We are literally split between our fearful ego (the little us) and our True Selves (the expansive us that is connected to the Source). The ego mind, with its limiting beliefs, is battling to remain in charge and to keep us in fear, because it knows that when we discover our True Self, it will be eclipsed.

The mass consciousness is the sum total of all the beliefs we are believing right now on Earth, and many of these beliefs are lies, keeping the vibration of the mass consciousness low. As each of us awakens and becomes aware, letting go of the old lies and allowing in the truth, this vibration ascends. As we each individually become aligned with the truth, we each create our own ripple effect in the world, because every relationship we have, whether it be with another human being, our work, our abundance or the Earth, will be transformed.

Our Earth is a living organism and its heartbeat, also known as the Schumann Resonance, is speeding up. This can be seen in the rate of change that has gradually increased over the past two millennia, with innovation transforming at great speed in the 20th century and at even greater speed this century. Developments in technology and the way we communicate are getting faster and more diverse exponentially, and some of us are finding it difficult to keep up. We, as human beings, are being challenged like never before to transform. Our old ways of existing are no longer working for us. There is an epidemic of anxiety and depression. It is only through an inner transformation process that we can adapt to a rapidly changing world.

## The True Self

True fulfilment cannot be sourced from our fearful, limited "thinking" ego mind; it can only be found from within our True Self, which is connected to the Source.

The Source has many names – The Universe, God, the Superconscious or the All That Is. Many of us have been turned off the word "God" because we have felt betrayed by our religion or church – in some religious institutions, power and control crept in, just as the ego mind creeps in on each of us, disguising itself as love. However, spirituality is not a religion. Deciding not to believe in this Greater Source because we have felt let down by a religion is like throwing the baby out with the bath water! The Source has always been there, will always be there, it is unconditional and it is love. When we are not connected to the Source, seeing it as separate to us, our ego is in charge, filling us with fear and creating from that vibration.

The Source is not separate from you. It is the whole and you are a part of it. It is holographic, so it is also a part of you. It is a divine matrix of energy and an infinite channel of love and pure potential. It is from this Source that we receive divine inspiration and the ability to create all that serves us in a positive and fulfilling way. It is from this Source that we can expand to our full potential in this life time – and create Heaven on Earth.

**You are a creator, not a victim**

We must now let go of the victim archetype, created by the ego mind, and open up to knowing that we are creating everything. No longer does it serve us to blame other people, circumstances or events for what isn't working in our lives, for no one has created our circumstances except ourselves. Blame is believing that someone is "wrong". If we believe others are to blame, we are believing a lie, and we are doomed to keep re-creating the past. Blame is a sure way of staying in a problem. No one is to blame, because every person is acting out of their own level of awareness and current vibration, including their own self-limiting beliefs. If you have been hurt or disappointed by someone, that person came into your life to reflect back to you a lie that you are believing about yourself. The vibration of that lie attracted the person or situation to you. If you didn't believe the lie, the person or situation would not have been manifested.

Not only is there no reason to blame others; there is no reason to blame ourselves, as any beliefs, thoughts, choices and actions up until now were chosen by our level of consciousness at the time. There is a difference between blaming ourselves and taking responsibility. By blaming ourselves, we are saying that we are 'wrong" which prevents us from loving ourselves. When we take responsibility, we acknowledge that we created something, and we also have compassion for ourselves.

## You've got to feel it to heal it

Many of us have cut ourselves off from our feelings because we don't want to feel emotional pain. We may have been conditioned to believe that pain is "bad", and so we deny our pain, and push it away, but if pain is not accepted and felt, it cannot be released. Pain is a message and it is neither right nor wrong, good nor bad. In our modern society, we have been told to "think positively", and discouraged from feeling our emotions, in the belief that we are somehow weak if we feel them or show them. The opposite is actually true – strong people feel and express their emotions, weak people block and deny their emotions. To truly understand ourselves, we must learn to feel. When the ego mind is in the driving seat, we can become numb because it judges emotional pain as "bad" and will do anything to resist feeling it. This resistance keeps emotional pain locked in us. In order to heal, we must be willing to feel our emotions. By doing this, we allow them to process and move through us. Have you ever allowed yourself to feel your emotional pain deeply? Have you experienced the shift that happens after a good cry? Very often you will feel lighter and freer. Some of us have had the experience of "hitting rock bottom" – the experience of feeling true despair. This is transformation working in us at a deep level.

***"Despair is the necessary prerequisite for the next degree of consciousness"***
***– Ram Dass***

If we have repressed our emotions for a long time, we may not be aware of what lies beyond the embracing of pain. We may be conscious enough to know whether we feel "good" or "bad", but for many, we've denied so many of our feelings that we are unable to discern what they are. This is particularly true for men because of social conditioning. Some of us are perpetually anxious, angry, frustrated or depressed and have no real understanding of why that is. We hold grief that has never been allowed to express itself, and it has become locked inside of us, creating stress, depression, anxiety and illness.

## The importance of self-awareness

Self-awareness is the bridge between the ego mind and the True Self. Awareness is our full attention to the present moment. When we are aware, we know that we have an internal life going on inside of us and that this internal life has a relationship with our outer life. Self-awareness is a state of being in which we are present and connected to ourselves as well as what is happening in our outer world. We are the observer and our life is the movie. This is also known as a state of mindfulness. It is the opposite of being on "auto-pilot" in which there is a density, because there is no observer. On auto-pilot, we are "fused" to our outside world without any awareness of self. It is only through this state of being aware that we create the space to observe ourselves and begin to understand ourselves. From this state of awareness we can choose our responses, instead of reacting unconsciously, and so we create positive and lasting change in our lives.

In this state of self-awareness, we can watch the "movie" of our life being played out – and it is being played out just for us, reflecting back to us all our beliefs, thoughts and feelings. Every situation, every person, every event comes into our life to show us something, and we have created it all either consciously, unconsciously or at the soul level for our personal growth. Without self-awareness, we cannot create the space to observe, and are doomed to a non-transformational life.

### Achieving self-awareness

Here are six simple ways to begin bringing self-awareness into your life. Whichever technique or techniques appeals to you right now is what is right for you.

- **Practise presence and observation** – Whenever you can, become aware of the present moment – right here, right now – and simply observe it. Observe without thought and refrain from labelling anything. Set an alarm on your phone two or three times a day, or put a few signs around your home or work space with the word PRESENCE or NOW to remind you to make contact with the present moment.

- **Feel your body** – Become aware of your body. Feel your head, face, upper body, lower body and feel your feet on the ground. Feel into the inside and outside of your body. Sense your organs, feel your breathing. Your body is constantly talking to you. When you connect with your body, you disconnect from your ego-mind and its constant thoughts.

- **Meditate** – Sitting with yourself and observing whatever comes to your mind - your thoughts, emotions, fantasies, agitations, distractions - is a highly effective way to become self-aware (I provide a simple meditation technique next).

- **Pay attention to your breath** – Notice your in-breath and your out-breath. Notice how your diaphragm moves, the sensations on your nostrils, the way the air travels through your system. Set an alarm on your phone two or three times daily to practise for a few minutes.

- **Observe nature** – By sitting and observing nature, you are connecting in with the Source and observing divine balance. Practice pure observation without any labels or thoughts.

- **Yoga/exercise** – Undertake exercise in a self-observant way. Notice your breath, feel your bodily sensations, observe your thoughts. Stay present.

- **Do something creative** – Paint, write, build, decorate, sew, knit, garden, colour-in, play – whatever gives you joy, make some time to do it. You will naturally connect with the Divine Matrix.

***You may believe that you will find the answers Out There, but you won't. The Truth is within you!***

## Meditation

Meditation is a fast-track to self-awareness, as long as it is performed with detachment from any outcome. This is a challenge to the ego mind that is highly attached to outcomes! The ego mind believes that looking inwards is a waste of time. In its perennially fearful state, the ego tells us the lie that we're too busy to sit and do nothing. It would rather us keep looking outside of ourselves for our happiness, hoping that the new job, the new car or the new relationship will make us happy!

This is the first block to meditation - our ego mind convincing us that the inner journey is a waste of time, when the truth is quite the opposite. The inner journey is the only way out of our unhappiness. The inner journey is the way to bliss. However, you need not begin a meditation practice to benefit from this book. Self-awareness can be achieved in other ways, as I have formerly mentioned. The messages in this book *will* be more deeply enhanced if you begin a daily practice of meditation. No amount of written information will put you in touch with your True Self. It is only through your own experience that you will begin to connect with the True Self not just as a concept, but as a direct, immediate experience. There are many benefits to be gained from meditation:

- Mental clarity
- Greater intuition
- Decreased stress and anxiety
- Increased joy and happiness
- More energy
- Better sleep
- Better management of emotions
- Clearing of emotional blocks
- Improved physical and mental health
- Conquering addictions
- Inner and outer balance

If you make the commitment to go inward, be prepared to be met by your ego mind over and over again. Our ego mind has wired us in a particular way and it doesn't want to give up control easily. Thoughts, emotions, and agitation are just some of the ego mind's strategies to sabotage our meditation. We cannot destroy the ego mind because it is a part of us. It is pointless to go into battle with the ego mind because that is ego mind thinking! Instead we must transcend the ego mind by accepting it and learning to sit and become aware of it. The word "transcend" means to "go beyond". Our True Self is so vast, that when we come into contact with it, we can begin to observe our ego mind and see it for what it is. We realise that we thought we *were* the ego mind, when in fact we were something far greater all along.

Meditation isn't something that you can or cannot do. It is a process, and it doesn't matter if you sit for 20 minutes with a busy mind or if you sit for 20 minutes with a still mind. Your intention to meditate is what is important – you are making contact inwards, as opposed to outwards – and through this process you will begin to access your True Self. Accept that when you begin to meditate, your mind will be very busy. As you progress, you will have days when your meditation feels peaceful, even blissful, and other days when meditation will feel like a battle. Observation and acceptance are the key to any meditation.

Over the page is an example of a simple meditation practice you can do each morning for 20 minutes. You can meditate anywhere – in a chair, on a bus, under a tree, in bed sitting up or wherever works for you. Ensure that there will be as little interruption as possible. It is a good idea to set an alarm on your clock or phone so that you commit to the full 20 minutes. The ego mind may convince you to give up earlier than 20 minutes, but override this urge. The biggest block to meditation is committing to doing it!

## A SIMPLE MEDITATION PRACTICE

- Sit in a comfortable position with your back straight, either supported or unsupported, depending on what is comfortable. Some people prefer to sit on the floor cross-legged or in lotus position, while others would prefer a chair, particularly if their hips are stiff.

- Close your eyes and begin to feel the inside of your body, starting with the top of your head and working your way down to your feet. Become aware of the spaciousness inside your body, and notice where you are holding any tension or pain. Pay attention to the feeling. Feeling the body is a powerful way of disconnecting from the ego mind.

- Now allow yourself to become aware of the outside sounds. Listen to them for a minute without judgment.

- Begin to focus on your breath – pay attention to the in-breath and the out-breath for a few minutes.

- Your busy ego mind will be continually creating thoughts and feelings, agitation or physical discomfort. At times it may pull you into a fantasy or scenario in your memory, or start making plans for the future. Simply override these thoughts, feelings and fantasies by returning your attention to either the outside sounds or your breath. Do not try to push thoughts or feelings away. Allow them to be there while focusing your attention back on your breath or the outside sounds. Over and over again, you will be pulled into a thought. Whenever you become aware of this, re-focus on your breath or the outside sounds.

- Meet whatever comes up with neutrality and allow the space for it to be there. Observe it and let it go.

- Surrender to the present moment. – over and over again for 20 minutes.

***Now is the time to become aware. Life is pushing you to do so – every painful experience, disappointment, so-called failure or sadness – is pushing you towards the door of awareness and the truth. Are you willing to reach for the handle and open the door?***

# THE SEVEN BELIEFS

## THAT LIMIT LOVE, HAPPINESS, PEACE AND PROSPERITY

1. I'll be happy when …
2. My life would be better if it weren't for …
3. I am not enough
4. There is not enough
5. Love hurts
6. It's not safe to change
7. Life is a battle

# LIE NUMBER ONE

## I'LL BE HAPPY WHEN ...

### The Truth:

### I can be happy independent of circumstances

***True and lasting happiness doesn't come from a desired outcome. If you are relying on an outcome for your happiness, it will be short-lived. True happiness can only be found from within and it follows that this inner fulfilment will create your outer fulfilment.***

If we are believing that we are going to be happy when we get what we want, such as achieving career success, falling in love with the right person, making a certain amount of money or retiring, we are making our happiness conditional. We are believing that our reality determines how we feel, when the truth is that how we feel actually determines our reality. If we wish to have the things we desire, it is essential that we learn to be happy irrespective of our circumstances now. That is the only way to create the very things we want!

It is the nature of the ego mind not to be content with what we have now:

- I'll be happy when I get out of this traffic jam
- I'll be happy when I leave the office
- I'll be happy when I finish doing my tax return
- I'll be happy when I have something to eat
- I'll be happy when I finally go to bed!

There is a perennial sense of emptiness in the ego, and so it attaches itself to future outcomes for a sense of happiness. This isn't our fault - we have been programmed to think this way. Think of our ancestors who believed that life was hard, but there would be a reward at the end – even if you had to die to get it! The belief was that we must suffer through life so as to ultimately find happiness when we got to Heaven.

**Heaven is here now!**

In each and every moment we can either choose to be in heaven (love) or in hell (fear). How we are feeling in each moment is a vibration, and I am sure you know the difference between feeling anxious, empty and fearful to feeling peaceful, full and loving. The belief that we are going to be happy in some distant future is a trick of the ego mind, which likes to take us out of the present moment, convincing us that life will be better when we get "over there". However, the future is only another present moment, and if our ego mind is still having its way, it will be taking us out of that future present moment as well, fooling us about another future moment "over there"!

### What is happiness?

Many of us confuse happiness with more extreme feelings - elation, ecstasy, excitement - but these emotions are fleeting. They are not sustainable and can be addictive. If we make these emotions our primary goal, we will experience disappointment over and over again. For every high, we will experience a low. What comes up must come down. True happiness comes about when we are at peace with the What Is and living in the present moment. It is an underlying joyful vibration that can be present even while we are feeling other so-called negative emotions. Our modern world has conditioned us to believe that if we don't "feel good", there is something wrong with us. Many of us feel ashamed of feeling sad, depressed, anxious or lonely, but as I've said earlier, feeling these emotions allows them to pass through us, and we can then return to happiness.

### The present moment is all that we have and contains all that we need

Every present moment contains not only all that we need; it contains the seeds of bliss. We may not have exactly what we want right now, but we have all the resources within us to create it. If we fully immerse ourselves in the present moment, we have access to the divine intelligence. From this present moment space, we intuitively know what we need to do next.

If we immerse ourselves in presence during difficult times, answers, signs and opportunities to heal or guide us will present themselves to us. These can come in many forms such as a solution coming to mind, the right person turning up at the right time, an idea, a message in the form of something someone says, a written sign, a song, or an event – but we would never receive this intelligent guidance if we were not fully present and aware in the moment. Life offers us one opportunity after another, if we choose to be present and aware and open to seeing it.

### The past and the future rob us of the present moment

If you are experiencing circumstances that you do not wish to be in, it is an invitation from the Universe to deepen into the present moment, and not follow the fearful ego mind into a vibration of lack, victimisation or reactivity. The present moment is robbed by our ego mind's memories of the past or its worry about the future. This drains our energy in the present moment and disconnects us from the Source. The past has been and gone, and the future is not yet manifested. Now is all that there is. If we don't let go of the lies that were created in the past and the fear that they have created in us now, we will re-live the past over and over again and re-live patterns that we never break free from in the future. But it doesn't have to be like this.

When we learn to be truly present, letting go of the past and the future, and immersing ourselves truly in the here and now, in most instances we will find there is nothing "wrong" in the present moment. When we learn to let go of the story that our ego mind wants to tell us about what is happening, we will discover in that present moment, that all is well. Most of what is "wrong" is purely a concept in our mind! Yes, we may feel sad, disappointed or angry – that may be what we feel in the present moment – but we do not need to add to it by churning up memories of the past or imagining a bleak future. The story of my client, Anna, is a good example.

Anna had struggled financially all her life, believing she would be happy when she made a certain amount of money, and feeling anxious because she hadn't. Not surprisingly, this very vibration created financial scarcity in her life. The only jobs she was offered were low-paying ones. She came to see me after she was made redundant for the third time.

"I've lost my job, my bank account is nearly empty, my rent is in arrears and I've got a limited amount of food in the cupboard," she told me. Naturally she was worried about her future. I invited her to "come into the present moment" and to become aware of her breath, and feel into her body.

"Right here, right now, is there anything to fear?" I asked.

"Yes!" she said "I don't have a job and –"

"That's just a thought, a concept. Right here, right now, is there anything to fear?"

"No."

"Can you see how the ego takes over and so the present moment is drained of any possibility? There is no possibility for answers while you're in fear."

Anna and I did a meditation together to calm and ground her. While her ego was controlling her, there was no presence and no awareness, but when she became present, she opened a space for inner peace.

"Now let's talk about your reality, right here, right now," I said. "You have an apartment to live in at the moment, there is some money in the bank and some food in the cupboard. Right now you have all that you need."

"Yes, but why does this keep happening to me?"

"Now you're going into the past. Let it go. It's been and gone. Just focus on the here and now … "

"I never did like that job. The hours were very long and I didn't feel respected by my boss."

"Anna, I believe that the Universe is always on our side and that everything that happens to us is for a good reason."

"Do you think the Universe pushed me out because there's something better for me?"

Now we were on the right track. Beginning to feel more accepting and peaceful, Anna and I went on to talk about the unfavourable aspects of her last employment so as to get clarity about what she did not want, and from that we worked on what she did want. We then "brainstormed" the many possibilities available to her. In the present moment, feeling calm, Anna got creative. I also suggested that Anna research what financial help she could find in the interim and to write a list of all the "positives" about being unemployed. She was surprised how long the list was! She had free time to do the things she never had time to do, but she hadn't realised this because she had been in fear. I then suggested she practise gratitude every day for the opportunity she had, and while feeling in this happy state, look for a new position that was more in alignment with her values. It didn't take her long to find a more fulfilling role.

In stressful times, we can either allow our ego mind to take us to the past or future and drain the present moment of its power, or we can choose to deepen into presence in this moment and reap the bounty that it contains. From this place comes the inner guidance of what we need to do next.

## Facing fear

Many of us are living in fear and have been in this vibration for so long that it has become our "normal" way of being. Underlying many lives are unexamined fears, but just because they are ignored doesn't mean that they are not sitting in our energy field. They are! When we deny our fears, we build a protective shell around ourselves and manage our lives by attempting to control everything – ourselves, other people and situations - so that we feel safe. When we live in fear, our world becomes smaller, because we don't want to face anything that triggers our fear, remaining in our "safety zone", unaware that we are getting stuck. If we no longer wish to live in fear, we must first become aware of it.

Fear is a powerful vibration that attracts to us the very things we fear. If we fear not being successful, not finding love or having enough, we block these things from manifesting; in fact whatever we think about while in the vibration of fear, we are in the process of creating it! This explains why "bad things happen to good people". Fear puts us in the vibration of scarcity. Worry and anxiety are powerful creators, drawing to us all that we are worried and anxious about. We can only create and attract what we desire from a place of inner peace. This is the vibration of love.

We cannot let go of fear by denying we are fearful. Instead we must shine a light on our fear. If you are feeling anxious, ask yourself what is the fear? Some of the most common fears are:

- Fear of poverty or not having enough
- Fear of abandonment
- Fear of being alone
- Fear of rejection
- Fear of dying
- Fear of failure
- Fear of intimacy
- Fear of humiliation
- Fear of change.

Being willing to look at your fears takes courage, but the very act of doing this and owning your fears begins to take their power away.

**Loss**

Most fears are based on the concept of losing or not having something. On the earthly level, loss can be painful. The ego mind doesn't want to lose anything; it cannot accept that loss is a part of life, and that we are in an eternal cycle of loss and gain. The ego wants to cling to everything it judges as positive. The True Self knows that life is a stream, allowing in and letting go, and that nothing is permanent. Things flow into our lives as we need them and out of our lives when they are no longer needed – people, possessions, money, opportunities – everything. It is normal to experience feelings of deep grief when experiencing a severe loss, such as someone we love passing away. Problems begin if we remain so dense in grief that we cannot allow in any light – we believe that because we feel sad, we cannot feel joy. We hold onto the sadness because we cling to the sense of loss, in the belief that we are somehow less than we were before. As long as we hold onto this sense of "diminishment", we block any new gains from flowing to us.

### Letting go allows in the new

The more willing we are to face our fears and let go of the old, the more we open ourselves up for the new. Many of us get "stuck" because we are unwilling to let go of something that is no longer serving us, or refusing to accept a loss we didn't want. Then we wonder why our lives are not improving or changing in positive ways. Like cleaning out a cluttered cupboard of old unnecessary things so as to re-stock it with what we need now, we must not cling to the old and outdated, because there will be no room for the new. No profound and positive change can come into our lives unless we are willing to let go. If you have experienced a profound loss in your life that you have found difficult to accept, allow the space to understand that you chose this on a soul level in order to learn the lesson of letting go.

## Beware of expectations

It is the nature of our ego mind to have expectations. The ego mind anticipates situations and events and if they fail to happen, we can plummet into feelings of disappointment, anger, bitterness, frustration and other toxic emotions. Whenever we are in the vibration of expectation, we are living in an illusion created by the ego mind that has attached itself to a desired outcome. The lie of expectation will be reflected back to us over and over again in the form of disappointment until we let go of expectation and accept the What Is.

## Accepting the What Is

Accepting the What Is means allowing the present moment to be what it is going to be! It doesn't mean that we give up on our hopes and dreams, but it does mean that we hold them "lightly in the palm of our hand". We can think "Wouldn't it be nice if …?", but we no longer need to think "I'll be devastated if it doesn't happen". By accepting the What Is, we come into alignment with the present moment. In this alignment, we can feel peaceful.

## Beware of "should"

Whenever we think or say the word "should", our ego mind will be involved. The ego mind thinks circumstances "should" be a certain way, other people "should" behave according to its judgments, and we "should" do something based on unconscious beliefs that are not necessarily true. When we think in terms of "should", we are in resistance to the What Is.

**Beware of comparison**

The old saying *"Comparison is the thief of joy"* is certainly true. Many of us compare ourselves and our lives to others', which inevitably creates unhappiness. Because the ego mind constantly wants "more", it will usually compare us to those it perceives to have "more" as opposed to those who have "less", disrupting our sense of appreciation for what we already have. Furthermore, the ego mind will only compare through a very limited lens – "she makes more money than I do" or "he has a wonderful partner and I don't" - it does not comprehend the whole picture, or consider that the other person may have challenges that are not on our ego mind's radar. This can place us in victim mode, believing that life is unfair. We each have a unique soul journey that contains unique soul lessons (challenges), so it is futile to compare ourselves with anyone else.

**We can choose to be happy, even if others are not happy**

I recall seeing a quote written on a date calendar years ago *"A mother is only as happy as her unhappiest child"*. "How true!" I thought. If we are empathic, we can fall into the lie of thinking "How can I be happy when there is so much suffering in the world?" or "How can I be happy when my partner/child/parent is unhappy?" If someone close to us is suffering, we may even feel guilty if we feel happy. These thoughts and feelings are based on a lie – that our happiness is conditional on others' happiness. If we believe this, we take ourselves to the lower vibration of the other person, and from this vibration we are unable to help or inspire that person. The truth is that we can feel joy and still empathise. Empathising does not mean that we must feel the way the other person does; simply that we go to the place of understanding how they feel. When we remain in a higher vibration of happiness, we access resources that are not available to us when in a lower vibration, and so we are better able to help another person who is unhappy. On a global level, each individual's level of happiness contributes to the overall vibration of the Earth, so it is essential that we choose happiness.

## Letting go of the fairytale

Most of us grew up reading fairytales and deep in our psyche, we still want to believe in them and "live happily ever after". As children we were led to believe that at some point, everything will turn out right and we will exist in continuous happiness for the rest of our lives. This is not possible! Not only would be this be very boring after a while; we would stop growing and expanding and finding new adventures. Do you have a fairytale you still want to believe in? The truth is that for every dream we manifest, we will create both the positive and the negative aspects of it. The dream home still needs cleaning, the ideal marriage will inevitably have its problems and the perfect family will eventually disappoint. There is a ritual I do with my clients where I ask them to write their fairytale, and then we burn it! When we let go of the fairytale, and no longer aspire to it, a miracle occurs. We allow our life to be what it is going to be – an authentic and meaningful life.

***"We must let go of the life we planned, so as to have the life that is waiting for us."***
***– Joseph Campbell***

## Gratitude

Gratitude is appreciating and loving all that we have now. When we are appreciating every moment, we are living it deeply and making the most of it. Gratitude is a feeling state. An attitude of gratitude knows that "here" is no better than "there". In fact, if we don't like being "here" and are not appreciative for what we currently have, we probably won't be in gratitude when we are "there" because we have not mastered the art of gratitude. Gratitude is a state of being that can be found within us in any situation. Not being able to live in gratitude is true poverty. Whatever we focus our attention on expands. The more we feel gratitude for what we already have, the more we will be given to appreciate. The more we focus on what we do not have, the more scarcity we create. If we take the time to sit and list all that we are grateful for, a profound shift occurs.

We switch from a vibration of lack (fear) to a vibration of abundance (love) and we feel different, and it is this feeling that switches on true happiness.

**You, and only you, can create your happiness**

When we rely on outside circumstances and other people to create our happiness, we are on shaky ground, because outside circumstances and people change constantly. That is the nature of our Universe. It is not what happens to you or doesn't happen to you that creates your happiness. No person or event can make us happy or unhappy. Our ego mind's judgments of the person or event makes us happy or unhappy. How we choose to interpret what's happening, and the story we tell ourselves about it, makes us happy or unhappy.

***"The last of human freedoms – the ability to choose one's attitude in a given set of circumstances."***
***– Viktor E. Frankel***

Too often we blame other people or circumstances for our lack of happiness. Difficult relationships reflect back to us what we must heal in ourselves. Very often, when we transform how we feel, the other person will transform too. In any relationship, the waters won't always be calm. By assuming responsibility for our own happiness, we are no longer at the mercy of other people's moods or choices. The people in our lives are limited by their own beliefs, fears and personal challenges, and how they behave is not a reflection of who we are. It is a reflection of who they are. How we feel about their treatment of us is a reflection of what we truly feel about ourselves. Throughout this book, we will be examining this further.

### There is no point in chasing happiness

Happiness cannot be chased. It is not a commodity, although the media will try and have you believe otherwise. Happiness is a by-product of a life well-lived, and tends to "sneak in through the back door". We cannot expect happiness from our relationships, our work or any situation or event, because our happiness is nobody else's responsibility but ours. When we start taking responsibility for our own lives and release the idea that other people or things are supposed to make us happy ... we will be happy!

### Inspired action

One of the greatest steps we can take towards our own happiness is to make choices that are in alignment with the things we truly want. Look inside your heart and ask yourself:

- What is it that truly matters to me?
- What do I value the most?
- What would I like my life to be about?

- Who do I want to be?

Whatever the answers, take a step towards the vision you have for your life, no matter how small that step is. If, for example, you wish to change your career and do work that you love, enrol in a part-time course that supports that dream or talk to someone who may be able to give you good advice or coach you on how to achieve your dream. If you want to meet your soul mate, create a vision board that expresses your relationship hopes and dreams and love yourself the way you would like to be loved. If you want to own your own home, create a vision board and start a savings plan. When we choose actions that are in alignment and moving towards what our True Self desires, we sow the seeds of happiness.

Conversely, if we constantly deny our hopes and dreams by choosing actions that are moving away from them, we will be sowing the seeds of unhappiness. The ego mind may prevent us from following our heart's desires with fearful thoughts such as "you'll never succeed", "you're dreaming", "you're wasting your time" and "it will never happen". When we make a step towards an inspired vision or a desire, it is the beginning of a process that contains infinite potential for our happiness and fulfilment, and as we commit to sowing the seeds of happiness, the Universe will step in and co-create with us in ways we could never have dreamed of.

***"Until one is committed, there is hesitancy, the chance to draw back, always ineffectiveness.***

***Concerning all acts of initiative (and creation), there is one elementary truth, the ignorance of which kills countless ideas and splendid plans: that the moment one definitely commits oneself, then Providence moves too. All sorts of things occur to help one that would never otherwise have occurred. "***
***- Scottish Himalayan Expedition***

## Journey not destination

Life is a journey – a process – and not a destination. The ego obsesses about the destination, which ensures continued unhappiness because we haven't reached our destination yet; the True Self loves the journey and revels in the mystery of it all. Bob, a man in his late 80's, expressed to me during a session that life had felt more enjoyable while he was on the way to achieving his dreams; once he got there, he wasn't as happy as he thought he would be. It was the *process of getting there* that he enjoyed the most. Of course, we never really "get there" anyway, because it is the ego mind's nature that once we achieve anything, it wants more. The whole of life is a process – a journey – and happiness is the vibration through which we choose to travel. Love the journey! It is so much more fulfilling than the destination.

## Sowing the seeds of happiness

We sow the seeds to our own happiness by:

- Accepting the What Is
- Assuming responsibility for our own happiness
- Letting go of the past and future
- Being present and aware of our thoughts and feelings
- Facing our fears
- Letting go of expectations, "shoulds" and comparisons
- Practising gratitude
- Taking inspired action towards our dreams
- Choosing to enjoy the journey regardless of the outcome.

**The paradox**

We can have hopes and dreams AND we can also choose to be happy whether or not we achieve them. Attachment to an outcome is the ego mind saying "I can't be happy unless I have this." The True Self says "I would like this very much but I choose to be happy whether or not I have it".

**To be aware of:**

Become aware of your happiness barometer. Are you feeling presence in this moment? Are you feeling inner peace and gratitude? Or are you feeling fear and scarcity? Accept whatever you are feeling and allow yourself to feel the feelings. Are you focusing on the past or the future? Are you overly-attached to an outcome or desire (wanting it too much)? Notice any thoughts that are taking you into a "lack" vibration. Remind yourself that you can choose to be fully present now, and that in this very moment you have all that you need. Become aware of all that you are grateful for in this present moment.

**Affirmations**

I choose to be fully present and here now.

I choose to become aware of my fears.

I choose to become aware of my worries about the future.

I don't need to allow fears from the past or worries about the future to rule my life.

I release and let go of all expectations and accept the What Is.

I release and let go of all "shoulds" and accept the What Is.

I release and let go of the need to compare myself and my life to others.

I release and let go of any need to blame other people or circumstances for my unhappiness.

I release and let go of any negative thoughts and feelings I have towards others.

I release and let go of any negative thoughts and feelings I have towards myself.

I choose now to be grateful for all that I am and all that I have.

All that I need I have now.

I surrender to the Source all my hopes and dreams.

I now move towards my hopes and dreams by taking inspired action towards them.

I trust in the Source to provide me with all that I need.

I release and let go of all attachment to outcome.

I now choose to be happy independent of my current circumstances.

# LIE NUMBER TWO

## MY LIFE WOULD BE BETTER

## IF IT WEREN'T FOR …

### The Truth:

**By accepting and embracing the challenges in my life, I surrender to my true path and complete my soul's purpose**

***The challenges you face are the keys to realising your full potential. Stop wishing they weren't there!***

Have you ever noticed how often you judge the events that happen in your life?

- I'm ill – *that's bad*
- He asked me to marry him – *I'm so happy!*
- I lost my job – *that's terrible*

- I won the lottery – *how wonderful*
- She left me – *that's devastating*
- I'm going on vacation – *that's fantastic!*

And yet, so often in hindsight, we gain a different perspective of these events.

- If I didn't get that illness, I would never have stopped and changed my life
- I didn't realise what I was getting myself into when I married him
- If I didn't lose my job, I wouldn't have started my own business
- I won the lottery but lost all my friends
- After she left me I met the love of my life
- The vacation was fun, but now I'm back and nothing has changed.

## The ego mind judges everything

Our fearful ego mind looks through a limited lens, labelling everything as positive or negative, good or bad, right or wrong. It cannot see the spiritual big picture or the spiritual "Why", nor does it know that whatever we are experiencing right now is an important part of our life mission. Judgment – whether negative such as criticism and dislike of self, others or circumstances, or positive – becoming attached to and idolising ourselves, a person or a circumstance – prevents us from seeing things clearly. Rather than judge, we must learn to observe things at face value and accept the What Is, because the truth is that no matter what happens to us, there will be both a positive and a negative aspect to it.

***Nothing is ever as good or as bad as it appears to be!***

Most of us have some idea about how we would like our lives to be. Some of us are goal-setters, some of us have a rough idea or a vision for ourselves and some of us just meander through life and live it on a more daily basis. However we choose to be, our ego mind has an intention, and that is for things to go according to its plan. From the ego mind's perspective, anything that happens that we didn't want to happen, or seemingly prevents us from having our desires met is seen as a block or a problem. When a challenge arises, we can feel frustrated, upset, sad, grief-stricken, impatient, disappointed, hopeless or a myriad of other emotions. These emotions come from the vibration of fear.

"This is not how it's supposed to be!" says our ego mind, and from this thought come other thoughts such as:

- I've failed
- Why me?
- Not again!
- I knew this would happen!
- I must have done something wrong for this to happen
- Just when I think everything's fine, this happens!
- This isn't fair!
- I'm being punished
- I never get what I want
- Things never work out for me
- I never get it right.

Our ego mind resists the What Is, and when we resist anything, we go into battle with it.

**On the soul level we choose it all**

Inbuilt into our life, and every life, are challenges. This is because, on a soul level, we are here to evolve and become greater, and we can only do this by having the lies we believe challenged. Our beliefs, thoughts and actions to date have created many of our challenges, while some were created by our soul for our evolution. Challenges are our soul's way of bringing to our attention our self-limiting beliefs. Challenges arise to show us where we need to expand and grow, but it may not be where our ego mind chooses to expand and grow, because the ego doesn't like pain.

The ego mind is a control freak that has fixed ideas about what it wants and how we are going to get it. It is very attached to outcomes and sees anything that takes us off our course as troublesome, blocking our happiness and fulfilment. It cannot see that every challenge presents itself to us for our growth.

***"For a long time it seemed to me that life was about to begin – real life. But there was always some obstacle in the way; something to be gotten through first, some unfinished business, time still to be served, a debt to be paid. Then life would begin. At last it dawned on me that these obstacles were my life."***

***- Alfred D'Souza***

When we set about creating a desire (which each of us is doing every day in every moment - whether it be fulfilling a task or working towards longer term goals), we will manifest everything we need in order to create it, and this includes both so-called "positive" and "negative" experiences. The positive experiences are reflecting back to us where we are holding the truth and the vibration of love and are able to create, and the challenging experiences are reflecting back to us where we are holding limiting beliefs and fear that block our creativity. These challenging experiences are showing us where we need to grow.

My client Amy wanted to meet her life partner, but over and over again she would meet men who caused her pain. She was being sent these people to show her the lies she believed about love. Another client, Simon, wanted to become more abundant, but instead of creating wealth, he never had enough money. These experiences were there to show Simon the lies he believed about abundance. Jo longed for her family to be more harmonious and loving, yet the family members were in constant conflict. The family situation reflected back to her the lies she believed about creating connectedness.

When we realise we are experiencing a challenge so as to bring awareness to a lie, we can stand back from the challenge and say:

*I'm not sure why or how I created this, but I am willing to take responsibility for it. There is something from this experience that I am meant to learn and grow from.*

## Acceptance

We cannot change what we do not accept. Acceptance is the first step to transforming an unwanted challenge.

From the space of acceptance (non-resistance), we alter our vibration from fear to love. The vibration of resistance stops us from loving ourselves and the situation. The very switch to acceptance frees us from the toxic emotions that come from resistance. Acceptance is yielding, freeing and soft. Acceptance neutralises how we feel about the situation, and therefore how we feel about ourselves. You could liken this to switching our body chemistry from acid to alkaline. When we feel inner peace and love for ourselves and the "problem", we are far better able to resolve it than if we are feeling the toxic emotions associated with resistance, such as frustration, anger and fear. The very vibration of acceptance (love) contains the seeds to transform a problem, because from this place our perspective changes, and the energy pattern around the problem shifts. Attempting to solve a problem from the place of resistance (fear) will ensure we stay stuck in it.

***"We cannot solve a problem with***
***the same mindset that created it."***
***- Albert Einstein***

Jonathan had cancer, and, understandably, had grown attached to the idea that his life would be better if it wasn't for his illness.

"I know this is a stretch, but I want you to imagine that your soul created this situation for your growth," I said. I was surprised how quickly and easily Jonathan embraced this notion, and as we talked I saw a peaceful expression settle on his face for the first time. "In what ways have you grown because of the cancer?"

"I've learned to appreciate every day because I don't know how many I have left. I've learned to tell the people I care about that I love them. My wife and I are relating to each other on a level I didn't think possible and we have travelled and experienced many things we've wanted to do in the last year, because we just don't know how long I'm going to be here for," he replied.

"They are very valuable lessons you've embraced. Can I suggest you do something?" I asked Jonathan to meditate and to send love and gratitude to his cancer. He does this now every day and his health has not declined further.

**Every challenge is showing us where we are withholding love**

We are not here to perfect our lives or ourselves. We are here to perfect our understanding of love. Challenges that show up in our lives reveal where we need to grow our understanding of love. Throughout my own life, I had a pattern of attracting angry people – people who would explode in anger violently and suddenly. I felt victimised from the angry explosions. Even when I left an angry person, the challenge would show up again in the form of another person! Finally I had to accept that there was something in me that was attracting this challenge. When the blindfold came off and I saw the anger I carried within myself, it was the beginning of my healing. Wherever we are holding toxic emotions – fear, anger, guilt, shame to name but a few – we are blocking love. We can deny and hide the parts of ourselves we don't like, but they remain with us whether we like it or not. Every challenge in your life has something important to tell you.

**If you refuse to learn the lesson from the challenge, it will keep showing up in your life in different forms**

Have you ever noticed that certain themes or patterns keep showing up in your life? This is because you are still in resistance to the real lesson that is being presented to you. Every time we realise the root of the challenge that dwells in us – and this will be a deep-rooted belief – and do the necessary work to release it - our potential expands in monumental ways, bringing outcomes often far greater than what we could have ever perceived.

Sarah was being bullied by her boss. Other people in the past had also made her feel stupid and inept and would put her down in front of other people.

"Tell me about your childhood," I said. "Did you ever feel the way you feel with either mum or dad?"

"In my mother's eyes I was never good enough. She would criticise me and humiliate me."

"Sarah, you are being given another opportunity to heal this wound. You may as well take this opportunity, because it is only going to keep happening until you do. Can you see that at the subconscious level your boss reminds you of your mother? And you fall into the vibration of fear and, understandably, feel anger and shame, because once again you are feeling not good enough? The more you believe and feel this, the more you attract this bullying treatment from your boss. Can you see this?"

## The lesson is more important than the outcome

Learning the lesson behind a challenge is more important than achieving any desired outcome. When the lesson is learned, it ceases to create future challenges that would have been created had the lesson not been learned. So while we can desire certain outcomes, we must balance creating our desires with the deeper lessons that life presents to us. This is true grace. The lesson behind the challenge is a valuable gift from the Source, even if we cannot see it yet, because when we heal the part of ourselves that created it, we expand in love, our energy changes and we allow in more light.

## The Dark Night of the Soul

There is a phenomenon known as the Dark Night of the Soul. Many people experience it on the transformational journey - a time or times in our lives where we may feel deep despair. During this period, it seems that we are continually challenged and experience a profound sense of loss. Although we may feel deeply depressed, lost, alone and desperate, spiritually, a great transformation is taking place. Why must we experience such suffering? Because at some point in our lives, we called it forth. We may have thought "I want to be happy!", "I want to be free!", "I want to live a life that is true to me!" The Source heard the call and set the wheels in motion for us to be transformed. We cannot transform without loss – we have to let go of the old in order to bring in the new. The process of transformation can be acutely painful. The Dark Night of the Soul is our old self dying, so that a New Self can be reborn. During this period, we are challenged to find resources within us that we would never have known we had unless we had this challenge. We seek new qualities within us in order to survive.

During my Dark Night of the Soul which lasted for over a year, I realised I could only live on a daily basis because I was too lost and confused to make plans. The art of presence is often a gift we receive during this time. Spiritually, a re-wiring is taking place. We cannot be the person we want to become unless there is a complete change to our energy circuitry. Think of an electrician re-wiring an old house. He cannot re-wire it by repairing the old wires. They are already aged and broken. He must pull out the old wiring and apply new wiring in a more updated and innovate way to meet the household's current requirements.

I had no idea at the time that this period in my life was leading to an unforeseen transformation, and that I would be doing the work that I am now doing. Life really is a mystery, and challenges really can be our greatest transformer.

## Forgiveness

On the earthly level, negative events can feel extremely painful and unfair, and so no amount of logic and reason is going to bring inner peace. It is only by viewing these events from a higher perspective that we can extract any meaning out of them, and even then we may not. If we are seeing the situation through the earthly lens only (the ego mind), our pain and sense of victimisation will remain, creating a vibration that will attract even more negativity. Alternatively, if we can view what happened as a soul choice – our soul chose to go through this experience in order that we expand and become greater – we can then we step onto the path to acceptance and forgiveness.

We must, however, embrace all the emotions that arise from the experience. It is normal to feel the emotions of grief, anger, despair and even a desire for revenge. We need not push these feelings away, but rather accept them, feel them and then be willing to let them go. We do not need to act on the desire for revenge for history has continually shown us the result of the ego mind's reactions – the re-creation of a similar vibration returning to us. As long as our ego mind is in control of us and demands justice, we will block the natural Universal Justice that exists. When we forgive, we release the toxic energy within ourselves that has been blocking the Universal Justice from flowing forth - also known as karma.

Forgiveness is acceptance, not approval. It is letting go of resistance and it is one of the most difficult things a human being can achieve, particularly if they are experiencing the emotions of hatred and revenge. Forgiveness requires us to open our hearts, and to no longer judge the offending person or circumstance. We may not like what was done to us or what happened to us and we don't have to think it was okay. To forgive, we accept what happened and we consciously choose to let go of all toxic emotions we hold towards a person or event, because if we don't let them go, the toxic emotions will hurt us.

Most of us have struggled to forgive at some stage in our lives. It is not uncommon for parents who have lost a child in tragic circumstances to feel they cannot forgive God, or for a person who has felt betrayed to stay feeling angry and vengeful for years. Forgiveness is a process and it is not one that we can force or fake. Our ego mind may try and tell us otherwise, but we can only know we have truly forgiven when we no longer hold any toxic emotions or feelings of revenge towards others or circumstances.

To begin the process of forgiveness, we must start with being willing to forgive. When we make that our intention, it will happen. Forgiving is the most powerful process we can undertake in this lifetime. Every situation that requires forgiveness is a gift from the Source for our transformation and expansion in love.

## The paradox

Even though we have the power to create what we want, we must embrace everything in our life; even those things that we perceive as not wanted or chosen by us.

## To be aware of:

When experiencing a challenge, take a moment to sit with the issue and do not rush to fix it. Become aware of your feelings. Allow them to be there, and feel them. Let go of all resistance to the challenge, reminding yourself that on some level you have created this and that you are meant to be experiencing this challenge in order that you learn and grow. Consciously choose to love yourself and the challenge. Say to yourself:

*I'm not sure why or how I created this, but I am willing to take responsibility for it. There is something from this experience that I am meant to learn and grow from.*

## Affirmations

I acknowledge and feel my feelings and fears around my challenge.

I release and let go of all resistance to my challenge.

I am willing and open to have a change of perspective.

I'm not sure why or how I created this, but I am willing to take responsibility for it.

I am willing to know that there is something from this experience that I am meant to learn.

I now embrace this challenge.

I know that this is an important part of my life journey.

I am willing and open to gain insights around this challenge.

I am willing and open to learn any necessary lessons from this challenge.

I choose to love myself and others throughout this challenge.

# LIE NUMBER THREE

## THERE IS NOT ENOUGH

### The Truth:

### In every moment there is enough

***True prosperity is not a place where you finally arrive. It is an ongoing process of following your bliss, and truly knowing that you are supported by a loving Universe that wants to provide the means through which to do it.***

The human race is ailing from a profound sense of lack, and yet we live in an infinitely abundant universe. Many of us believe:

- I don't have enough money
- I don't have enough time

- I don't have enough love
- I am not successful enough
- I am not attractive enough
- I am not happy enough
- There is not enough love in the world
- There are not enough resources in the world.

The ego mind believes in a limited world with limited resources. Abundance is often seen only in terms of money and things, but money and things are worthless if we have poor health, depression, poor relationships or no time to enjoy the moment. Contemplate the Earth's history for a moment; the mass consciousness has held the belief that there is not enough for a very long time, and we still do – and so we go on creating that reality. The belief is so imprinted within us, it creates continual thought spirals of scarcity. We are surrounded by this belief – fearful people, the media, organisations and governments – so it is not surprising that we go on believing it and creating it. Commercials like to convince us that there is something missing in our lives, so that we are driven to buy the missing thing. Many of us are still living in survival mode – doing work we don't like so as to pay for life's needs, putting up with unfavourable situations because we "need the money" and risking our health because of the stress. We have lost the knowledge that abundance is our divine right. When we were born to the Earth, automatically programmed into our being was providence. We live on an abundant earth which wants to provide for us in a divinely balanced way.

Because of our conditioning, it is the compulsion of the ego mind to focus on what we do not have, perpetuating a sense that there is always something missing. Many of us grew up in situations of scarcity, created from the concept that there is only so much to go around. The idea that there is not enough contradicts what our True Self knows to be true: that there is a continuous flow of abundance if we choose to know it is so. In any moment in time, there really is enough, or at least there is the potential to create enough. If you have struggled with "not enough-ness", it hasn't been created by the circumstances you were born into, or bad lack or any other earthly occurrences. These circumstances and occurrences were created by the belief that there is not enough.

## Abundance is a constant flow

If you look at nature, you will appreciate the abundance of the earth. Nature manifests in perfect harmony and balance. Grass doesn't try to grow; it just grows. Flowers bloom in divine timing and wither when their work (pollination) is done. Fruits and vegetables grow (mostly) in summer and are harvested in Autumn, and then the cycle begins again in Spring. Like nature, abundance is in constant flow. For each of us, if we choose to believe it, things will flow into our lives as we need them and out of our lives when they are no longer useful, and yet if you have been conditioned to believe in scarcity, not only will you find it difficult to believe this; you will not trust in the flow. Instead, you will want to cling and accumulate.

## Emptiness creates the desire for "more"

When we believe there is not enough and feel a sense of deprivation, our ego mind will crave the thing there is not enough of, wishing that we could have more. Our level of consumption gets out of balance. Contemplate for a moment the level of consumption in the world today:

- Overblown consumption, creating an over-abundance of things
- The increasing desire to own more things
- The building of bigger houses and the associated energy consumption
- More things being manufactured than ever before, and disposed of in landfill
- Food addiction, creating an epidemic of obesity and its associated illnesses
- Other addictions - drugs, alcohol, sex, internet, shopping, gambling - are on the rise.

When we believe there is not enough, we feel driven to seek things outside of ourselves to fill our inner-emptiness, but they are not the things that will make our lives any better in the long-run. The desire for more has created a polarising effect in the world. Many of us create more money and own more things, but we have less time and inner peace. Some of us have created what we thought was success – wealth, possessions and status - and yet we are not happy. The imbalance is also evident in the world at large. While some countries are highly affluent and have surpluses of all resources, other countries are ridden with poverty and have a deficit of the basic necessities. We have either become fearful of not having enough, and so we over-consume to compensate for that fear, or we genuinely do not have enough.

## Greed and the win/lose paradigm

The fearful vibration of greed brings out the worst in humanity – whether it is a greedy person at the dinner table, a corporate leader who ensures he gets paid thousands of times more than those employed by his corporation, or a country going to war over land or resources, greed says "There isn't enough, so I have to fight for my share and get as much as I can." Greed creates in us an ongoing experience of fear and the belief that we must gain, even if someone else loses.

The current win/lose paradigm of the business world manifests as corporations focusing entirely on profit, at the cost of people and the environment, rather than taking a holistic, balanced approach, based on a win/win paradigm that creates a profit, nurtures employees and gives back to the community and the earth. Many heads of corporations would say this vision would be impossible because their belief systems won't allow such a possibility.

**The more we desire and create from the ego, the less fulfilled we become**

From the lie that there is not enough comes the belief that "more" will fix our lives.

- The more money I have, the happier my life will be
- The more my partner gives to me, the more loved I will feel
- The more friends I have, the more I will feel loved
- The more my children succeed, the more successful I will feel.

Ironically, when we crave "more", the more elusive our happiness becomes because we are in the vibration of fear and scarcity. The ego doesn't know when enough is enough because it believes that the more we add to our lives, the more fulfilled we will be, even if past experiences have told us otherwise. When we create our lives based on the ego's desires, we may succeed at achieving those desires, but these things will not necessarily bring us lasting fulfilment. To use an extreme example, Hitler (a super-ego) was highly creative!

The ego convinces us that the next thing we desire will bring us happiness and fulfilment and when it doesn't, it will think of something else, leading us on a never-ending mission of short-term fulfilment followed by emptiness. If we are viewing our life through the ego mind, there will always be not enough of something.

- I am now successful, but I don't have enough time
- I'm wealthy, but I'm lonely
- I've found a husband, but he's not giving me enough attention
- I've had children but I'm not fulfilled
- We bought our dream house, but we don't have fun
- I left my wife for someone younger, but she nags me too
- I've achieved my goals, yet I'm not happy.

## Renunciation is not the answer

For some, a lack of fulfilment in outside things has led them to renounce them entirely. This is the pendulum swinging the other way – a belief that earthly pleasures are somehow bad. Renunciation is the basis of many religions, however it is not the "having" of material things or intimate relationships that bring us pain. It is the over-identification and attachment to material things and intimate relationships that brings pain. It is the *need* for them that brings us pain. While renunciation may feel safe, it fails to recognise the human being in us. We are spiritual beings having a human experience, and we have incarnated here to master being human and to learn to create our True Self's desires through our connection with the Universal Source. We are here to create and enjoy earthly pleasures – human connection, sexual union, our homes, food, art and things. These things are not evil, but rather, a part of the human earthly experience. They enhance our lives, but they are not supposed to fix our lives. They become bad for us if we are manifesting them in the belief they will make us whole – this is impossible because we are already whole. No amount of "things" will make us whole because they cannot fill the emptiness our ego mind has created.

## The answer isn't more or less; it's balance

The ego refuses to understand that we must pay for everything. Whatever we create, we will manifest both gains and losses. Everything is an exchange of energy and for anything that we desire and manifest, we will have to give something up. If we are intent on creating more, we will create both the positive and negative manifestations of that desire. The ego mind wants only to focus on the positives; it doesn't want to know about the negatives, but the truth is:

- The more we own, the more we have to take care of
- The wealthier we become, the greater the responsibility we have
- The harder we work, the less time we will have for our personal relationships
- The more time we invest in our personal relationships, the less time we have for our work
- The more children we have, the less time and resources we will have for ourselves
- The more marriages we have, the more complicated our families become
- The more we produce, the more resources we consume.

## Creating from the True Self

While the ego "consumes", the True Self creates. From the True Self, we exchange energy in order to transform it into something else. We are all creators and it is our divine nature to create, but not from our ego mind. Our True Self intrinsically knows what we really want and thinks in terms of "enough" but not "more". The True Self, connected to the Source and the Divine Matrix, manifests in a balanced way. Most of us want:

- Good health and wellbeing
- Work that we enjoy
- A sense of purpose
- Loving relationships
- A nurturing home
- Time to enjoy life and see beauty
- Fun and creativity
- Beautiful experiences
- The joy of giving and receiving
- A flow of income to enable us to have these things.

This is true abundance! When we get in touch with our True Self, we begin to know that we already have enough. Our True Self co-creates with the Source. It doesn't think in terms of "more" or "less". Our True

Self is always in the vibration of love and so it thinks in terms of inspiration and bliss, and whatever the True Self creates will be in balance with the rest of our lives.

### To create abundance we must feel abundant

We can only create abundance from an existing vibration of abundance. When we truly know and believe "I already have enough" and we feel ourselves and our lives to be abundant, we will continually attract further abundance. It is impossible to create abundance from the vibration of lack. This is the Universal Law of Attraction – like attracts like.

***"For to everyone who has, more will be given, and he will have an abundance. But from the one who has not, even what he has will be taken away"***
***- Matthew 25.26.30***

### Gratitude

Gratitude is the most powerful way to switch from a lack vibration to that of abundance. If you don't do this already, I suggest writing in a gratitude journal daily and noting all the things you are grateful for, or list these in your mind before or after a meditation.

### Accumulation Vs Abundance

The ego mind obsesses over the future, and worries that there will not be enough. It will have us believe that accumulation is abundance, and that we must strive for all that we can get right now, even if we don't like what we have to do or the pace we have to work at so as to get it. So great is our fear that the future will not provide for us, that we seek to create a nest egg to quell our anxiety about our future security. We literally sacrifice the present, in the hope of ensuring a happier future. While there is nothing intrinsically wrong with accumulating wealth and planning for the future, if we are doing this to the detriment of our health and happiness now, then we are deluding ourselves as to its value, because we may not be around to enjoy it!

In order to keep up with the changing Earth vibration, now more than ever we are being required to create in the present moment, and allow the future (another present moment) to take care of itself. Volatile stock markets, unreliable property prices and a changing world economy means that the old structures of financial safety that we have traditionally relied upon for our sense of security are no longer as reliable because of the increasing unpredictability in the world. This is an even greater reason to trust in the Universal Source that the right abundance will flow to us as and when we need it in a balanced and harmonious way, and we do not need to risk our inner peace and health for it. If we are working and earning at a pace that is making us unhappy or unwell, we will be taken out of the Universal Flow, and so our hard work and accumulation may amount to nothing.

Outside circumstances are pushing us evermore to live via our True Selves in the moment and trust in the flow. This does not mean that we should no longer make financial plans for the future, but in these changing times we must remain flexible and not be overly-attached to how our abundance comes to us in the future. By being fully present and in the Universal Flow now, we are creating our ideal future.

We must let go of the concept of "retirement" which is an unnatural phenomenon. Purpose is important to all of us, no matter what age we are. As we age, we may work less or change the work we do, but having a sense of purpose is what sustains our life force energy. There is no reason why we cannot continue to create our abundance in our older years.

**The Universal Law of Giving and Receiving**

The Universe operates through exchange – a circulation of energy - a divine balance of both giving and receiving. If we are continually expecting to receive without giving, we will feel disappointed by life. Conversely, if we are continually giving to others with no exchange or for very little in return, then we are not valuing ourselves, and the result will be that we will not be valued by others. If our pattern of giving or receiving is out of balance, our lives become out of balance. Giving and receiving are exchanges of energy. It is in our spiritual nature to give, but we must not give at cost to ourselves (sacrifice). Receiving is also a part of our spiritual nature, but we must learn to receive not at cost to another (selfishness).

Many of us have a pattern of either giving too much or taking too much. Both choices are not based on love. In most societies, we praise those who give too much and denounce those who give too little, but neither pattern is helpful to anyone ultimately. A pattern of giving too much will be based on believing that who we are is not enough and so we must give so as to make up for the deficit. People who give too much ("givers") tend to attract to them those who take advantage of their giving nature ("takers").

People who give too much often feel short-changed by life because they are uncomfortable with receiving, yet how can they receive the Universe's gifts unless they are open to receiving? Those with a strong pattern of taking are in fear that there is not enough, and so they take as much as they can get, hoping it will fill the emptiness. These people have a win/lose mentality and have no problem with receiving. They will seek out those who are givers and allow them to give until they are empty. But even then, they will believe that the giver hasn't given enough because they still feel empty.

If we give too much or too little, we take ourselves out of the Universal flow, because the flow is energised by giving and receiving in equal measure. If we have a habit of giving too much, our work is to hold back after giving, and allow time and space to receive. If we tend to give too little, our work is to start giving more and focus less on what we receive in return. Changing these habits can feel uncomfortable at first, so it is best to start to change the pattern in a small way, and as we gain confidence that we are going to be okay, we can build it up to greater levels.

When we learn to give and receive in balance, we attract to us people who also know how to give and receive in balance. If there is something that we truly desire and it keeps eluding us, we must learn to give it first. If there is something we dearly want to give but no opportunity arises for us to do so, we must learn to allow ourselves to receive it first.

The only way to give is unconditionally and willingly. If we are giving to another in the hope of receiving something in return, or attached to any outcome from making that gift, then it is not a genuine gift. It is, in fact, manipulation. If you feel unwilling to give or feel the need to put conditions on a gift, it is better not to give at all.

### When we believe there is not enough money

Money is a sensitive touchstone for many people. We may have grown up in families with beliefs like:

- Money doesn't grow on trees
- It's not good to be rich/wealthy people are bad people

- You have to work hard if you want to make money

- You can only be happy if you are rich

- Money is the root of all evil

- It's greedy to charge money or to have money.

These beliefs create a dysfunctional relationship with money. Whatever your relationship with money, it will be the same relationship you have with people, work and other domains in your life. For instance, if you are greedy for money, you will more than likely be greedy for love, recognition and things. If you believe it is greedy to have money, you will feel unworthy of money also feel of love, recognition and things. We all have a "money story" from which we create our abundance.

Money is simply an energy – a medium of exchange. Someone provides a service or product, and we give back to that person the value of the service or product. Exchanging money for goods and services is not only a necessary way of living in our modern world, it is a divinely right way of living, because it creates balance and flow. That is why money is often referred to as currency! When we believe there is not enough money we are going to either create a lot of money out of greed, or create very little money because we push it away. Let's take a look at the beliefs mentioned above, based on some of my clients' money stories.

**Money doesn't grow on trees** – Cathy grew up in a family who "just scraped by". She was often told "we can't afford it" when she wanted something. As an adult she struggled with having enough money. Even though she was now in well-paid employment, bills and other financial obligations created a vibration of scarcity in Cathy's life. There never seemed to be enough money to do the things she would like to do.

**It's not good to be rich/wealthy people are bad people** – Ian grew up in a family that believed it was somehow shameful to be wealthy, and that rich people were bad people. Every time he got a pay rise he would feel out of his comfort zone. An opportunity arose to be promoted, but he failed the interview. Secretly he suspected he sabotaged himself.

**You have to work hard if you want to make money** – Christina's family were Italian immigrants who worked hard to create a better life for their family. Even though she had more educational opportunities than her parents, she also inherited their work ethic. Now an accountant, she still believed that she must work very hard in order to make a living. Christina is a workaholic who struggles to live a balanced life. She makes good money but has no time. She is divorced because her ex-husband felt that she prioritised her work over their relationship.

**You can only be happy if you are rich** – Mike was ambitious. He grew up in a family who struggled financially and had decided, by the age of 12, that in order to be happy he would have to make a lot of money. This became his obsession over everything else. When I met Mike, he was a wealthy self-made man, but no matter how much money he made, it was never enough. Mike experienced constant anxiety about losing his wealth, because he believed that if he lost his money, he would lose his power and happiness. Ironically, he had already lost both anyway.

**Money is the root of all evil** – Gabi felt disappointed that her husband didn't buy her many gifts. I suggested she buy those things she desired herself. "I want him to give them to me," she replied. Gabi was a reasonably wealthy woman but didn't like handling money, believing it was somehow "dirty" or distasteful. Her husband paid the bills and took charge of the domestic finances while Gabi put her proverbial head in the sand and seethed with resentment that she wasn't given what she wanted.

**It's greedy to charge money or to have money** – Lily had begun working for herself as a healer. She came to see me because she was struggling financially. She charged her clients very little, and some she healed for free. "What you are charging is very low. Why don't you put your prices up?" I asked. She was sceptical, believing that if she was a spiritual person, it was wrong to charge money in exchange for healing. This is a common belief among healers. No matter what work we do, we must value ourselves, our skills and our time by exchanging a fair amount of money for our services. The more we value ourselves, the more others will value us too.

Whatever our early experiences were around money, and our parents' beliefs and attitudes, these will have created an impact on our relationship with money. Take a moment to contemplate your money story and the beliefs you inherited from your family. It is never too late to let these beliefs go!

Some of us resent paying bills, instead of rejoicing in our ability to pay for the services that enhance our lives. Every time you pay a bill, be aware that you are circulating money. When you help create wealth for others, you are also creating wealth for yourself, because whatever you give away will return to you.

A healthy relationship with money is a balanced one. An over-attachment to money will bring us unhappiness, as will an under-attachment to money. We need to value money and have a healthy respect for it, and to circulate it in positive ways by spending money and investing money on the things that truly matter to us and will enhance our lives and the lives of others. Not valuing and disrespecting money by "throwing it around" and using it in ways that do not ultimately serve us or others will ensure that we stay in lack.

**When we believe there is not enough time**

For many of us, life is a race against the clock. We may work in high-pressure environments or have busy families that run on tight schedules and we feel burdened and overwhelmed. We jam our diaries with meetings, activities and deadlines (believing we are achieving more), ticking them off as we go, waiting for a time in the future when we can reward ourselves and relax, but this rarely happens. If we believe there is never enough time, there never will be! This belief can be so entrenched that we cannot see we are creating our own busy-ness, and there is no space to see that there can be another reality. Observe how often you say "I don't have time". With every statement such as this you create the reality of not enough time. When we are racing through time, rarely do we slow down, deepen into the moment and feel its richness, nor do we engage deeply with other people. Instead, we skim the surface of life, never fully present and open to what that moment has truly has to offer.

Time offers us space to create and achieve, but many of us misuse time by attempting to cram too much into it! This is just another case of believing that "more" will make our life better, when in reality it robs us. Our True Self knows that there is always enough time, and if there isn't enough time for something, then it is not meant to be.

***"The butterfly counts not months but moments, and has time enough"***
***- Rabindranath Tagore***

To the ego, time is our enemy. To the True Self, time is our friend, because there is always enough time. We explore this subject further on in this book.

## When we believe there is not enough love

If our lives feel devoid of love, it is because we haven't yet found the endless source of love that exists within ourselves. We are believing that love is a commodity that exists elusively "out there", but the amount of love in our lives is a direct reflection of the amount of love we feel within. Underlying many human lives is the lie that there is not enough love. When we believe there is not enough love, we will focus on every situation where we feel unloved and from this we create a further scarcity of love. Feeling unloved is an invitation from the Universe to go within and ask ourselves "In what ways am I not loving myself enough?" and "Where am I not loving others enough?" When we begin to love ourselves and others more, we attract more love to us from the outside. Wherever we feel love is lacking in our lives, we must learn to give love first, and wisely remove ourselves from people and situations that are loveless. We have a whole chapter coming up, in which we explore love further.

## All our abundance comes from the Source

You may believe that your money comes from your salaried job, but in truth it comes from the Source. Your job is just the vessel through which it is channelled to you right now. You may believe that the love you receive from your partner, friends or children comes solely from them, but in actuality it comes from the Source. Perhaps you believe that the blissful events and enjoyable times in your life come from those particular times and events, but again, it is a gift from the Source. When we believe that our abundance can only come to us through particular channels, we close ourselves off from the infinite abundance. If we believe that the only money that can come to us is the money we earn from our job, we close ourselves off to the infinite possibilities that exist. If we expect that the only love we can receive is from a few key people in our lives, we close ourselves off to the limitless love that is all around us. If we believe that we can only find enjoyment in certain activities, we close ourselves off from so many other channels of joy. When we open ourselves up and declare "I am open to ALL of the channels of abundance" and let go of our limited perception of where our abundance should come from, we open ourselves up to miracles.

For years I struggled with a lack mentality, believing there wasn't enough money, time or love. Like so many of us, I was raised by parents who believed there wasn't enough money and it wasn't their fault. They were born during the depression and grew up during World War 2. The world was in a serious state of lack, so of course they would worry about money. Throughout my young adulthood and mothering years, there was never enough time. Looking back, I realise that most of my time was spent doing things that I "should" do, rather than things I truly wanted to do. I was never taught to love and value myself, so I looked for love and approval from the outside. Love from the outside remained elusive until I learned to truly love myself. This lesson wasn't learned until my late 40's. What I have learned is that the more I do what I know feels truly right and good and true, the more I am looked after by this abundant universe in every way.

**The Paradox**

We won't ever have enough until we believe we already have enough. If we want more, but we are in a vibration of lack, we will never create more. True abundance can only be manifested when we are in touch with our True Self and know that we already have enough

**To be aware of:**

Become aware of thoughts that there is not enough. You may be surprised just how often they come up. Notice the feelings that come up with these thoughts. Become aware of the stories that your ego mind is wanting to tell you. If you are feeling empty, stay with the feelings and drop the story. The emptiness is being caused by a lack of connection to your True Self. It has nothing to do with what you don't have. Remind yourself that you already have enough, even if your ego mind is convincing you that you don't. You live in an abundant Universe that wants to co-create with you. You have all the resources within you to create the things you desire, if they are aligned with your True Self. Allow yourself to move out of the vibration of lack and into the vibration of abundance by noticing all that you have in this moment, and create a gratitude list. Say Thank You to the Source for all that you have. Become aware of the abundance all around you – nature can remind you that abundance is in constant flow– the leaves on the trees, the flowers and the sunshine. You don't have to own abundance to feel it!

**Affirmations**

I am willing to release the lie that there is not enough.

I release and let go of all fear, worry and anxiety about not having enough.

I choose to know that right now there is enough and I am safe.

Abundance is my divine right.

I trust in the Source to provide me with all that I need right now.

I have the potential within me to create all that is in my highest good.

I live in an abundant Universe that delights in co-creating with me.

The Universe is on my side and wants me to live an abundant life.

I am open to all channels of abundance.

I act in my highest good now and I allow the future to take care of itself.

There is always enough money.

There is always enough time.

There is always enough love.

I already have enough and I am so grateful.

I choose to do what I know is right and good and true and I know I will be provided for.

# LIE NUMBER FOUR

## I AM NOT ENOUGH

### The Truth:

### In every moment I am enough

***You are so much more than you think you are. Every relationship and situation in your life is reflecting back to you what you believe about yourself.***

The belief we are not enough is a lie that lives to a greater or lesser degree at the very core of most of us and shows itself to us in every relationship and situation where we feel less than whole and happy. On a human level we are all faulty. There is no such thing as a perfect human being. When we can see the perfection in that, we no longer need to seek perfection in ourselves, and we can begin to know that who we are in any moment is enough. Our ego mind will tell us otherwise – poisoning the present moment with pain from the past and anxiety about the future. Our True Self knows that everything is in divine order and perfect just the way it is right now, and we are a part of that perfection. Where we are on our life journey is exactly where we are meant to be.

If we have made "mistakes", we were meant to make them so that we could learn, grow and become more. Instead, we listen to the ego and believe that we are somehow wrong and guilty. The lie that we are not enough was inherited from our families, our ancestors, our teachers and religions. Even when these people and organisations are no longer in our lives, the imprint remains; our own inner voice taking over with self-criticism, self-blame and self-loathing. How can we expect to be truly loved if we cannot love ourselves?

Wherever we are holding the belief that we are not enough, we will create relationships and situations that reflect this back to us, and in our unaware state, we see this as proof that we are not enough. From the belief we are not enough, come other beliefs:

**I'm not good enough** – we may have developed this belief from the way we were treated by key people in our life growing up. If our parents felt not good enough, we would have taken on those imprints. When we feel not good enough, we struggle to live life to our full potential. We see every negative or disappointing situation as further proof that we are not good enough, instead of seeing it as a learning experience that is reflecting back to us the need to change our belief. Because we are holding this lie, we feel inferior and give our power away when relating to others whom we see as "better" than us, or get angry and blame another person for not treating us well.

***The truth: If you have incarnated on this Earth, you are good enough.***

**I'm not worthy or deserving** – some of us experienced a scarcity of love, time or things when we were growing up. We may have been told by our parents "not now" or "we can't afford it" when we wanted or needed something; some of us were told we were selfish for having desires, and now we go through life feeling ashamed of wanting. We are then not able to manifest our desires because at the core level we don't feel worthy or deserving of them. Even if we are presented with opportunities, we will subconsciously sabotage them to create the reality we believe.

***The truth: You are here to learn how to create your desires and you are worthy and deserving of them.***

**I'm not important** – if we were neglected, ignored or felt unimportant as children, we will be triggered whenever we feel we are not being treated as a priority. If we believe we are not important, we will unconsciously create "unimportant" lives, be overly sensitive to how others are treating us, or create or attract situations where we feel we are a low priority or "second best".

***The truth: You are an essential and important part of the Universal whole. It wouldn't be the same without you.***

**I must work very hard to prove myself** – if the only way we could gain attention or feel loved as a child was by achieving, we were set up to become workaholics as adults. Workaholism is an addiction which destroys relationships and life in general. Deep down, a workaholic feels that they are "nothing" unless they are working hard and achieving. Workaholics struggle to maintain intimacy, lack innate joy and are highly likely to become depressed or physically ill. They find it difficult to stand still, relax and just "be".

***The truth: Your very presence here on earth is enough.***

**I'm a failure** – when we believe this, we see everything in our lives that failed as a reflection of who we are, instead of seeing each situation as a learning experience. While a task or effort may "fail" by not achieving our desired outcome, if we hold the belief that we are a failure, we take the event personally. Every time something fails, we add it to our list of past failures and reinforce the lie. We eventually give up on our hopes and dreams because we fear the next failure.

***The truth: Failures are a part of life, and we all experience failures on our way to success.***

**I can't** – whatever we feel we cannot do is a reflection of the lie that we are a limited being with limited potential. Our parents may have held this lie and passed it down to us through their words, thoughts and actions. This belief stops us from attempting anything new, and we become stuck and unable to expand and grow.

***The truth: You have all the resources within you to do anything you put your heart and mind to.***

**I'm not lovable** – if we didn't feel loved as children, we are likely to believe that we are not lovable, and so we will attract to us people who don't love us or people who do love us but we cannot recognise or accept their love.

***The truth: You are not only lovable; your very essence is love.***

**I must put others before myself** – most of us have been told that to put others before ourselves is a divinely noble thing. We were encouraged by our parents, our communities, our governments and our religions to put others first, and to sacrifice our own needs for the needs of others. This has been a belief in the mass-consciousness for a long time – think of martyrs and soldiers. From this lie we believe that if we give enough, we will become enough. Instead, over time we become drained, resentful and even bitter.

***The truth: By giving to yourself before others, you become more able to give to others in a greater, more energised and balanced way.***

**People always leave me** – many of us were abandoned, either emotionally or physically, when we were young. From this trauma we will hold a fear of further abandonment and then re-create it. This can be a deep wound where we don't feel intrinsically safe in relationships, swinging between clingy and detached. We then attract to us people who abandon us, or alternatively our fear drives us to act in such a way that creates further abandonment. If we haven't healed this wound, our lives will contain a pattern of people leaving us either physically or emotionally.

***The truth: People come and go. Whoever is meant to stay in your life will stay.***

**I'm alone and unsupported** – when we believe that we are continually alone and unsupported, we will search outside of ourselves for the connection we crave, hoping that a new relationship, friendship, community, thing or activity will give us the sense of connection that we are craving. We place a lot of expectations on relationships, hoping that another person will make us feel whole. The disconnection however, is actually with our Higher Self and no person, group or situation can give us that deeper sense of connection for long. This belief creates a neediness that actually repels others.

***The truth: When you are connected to your True Self, you will know that you are never alone and always supported.***

**I can't speak up for myself** – the inability to speak up for ourselves comes from earlier experiences when what we either asked for or said was ignored, put down or punished. We developed the belief that it was futile to speak our truth or to ask for something. As adults we gag ourselves, holding in frustration and resentment towards those around us, fearing that we will either be punished or abandoned if we say what we would really like to say.

We bottle up our truth, and then occasionally allow it to explode out of us in exasperation or anger, which ensures it won't be received or heard.

***The truth: You are here to speak your truth with love and you are worthy of being heard.***

**I must do everything perfectly** – if the outside world told us we were not good enough when we were young, we may feel the need to do everything perfectly and become hard task masters on ourselves and possibly others. Perfectionism expends a lot of energy and prevents us from taking risks because we fear the result won't be perfect,

***The truth: Mistakes and imperfections are necessary for your growth. You are perfect in your imperfection, and your best is good enough.***

**I'm stupid** – if we didn't fit into the school academic system, achieve good grades or were given the message that we were intellectually inferior, we may still believe deep down that there is something wrong with us and we are inferior and stupid. For too long humanity has prized only a narrow and limited type of intelligence – intellect – but this is just one type of intelligence. Divine intelligence is innate and present in all of us. If we believe we are not intelligent, we are unlikely to believe in our own gifts and therefore never find them, reinforcing the belief that we are stupid.

***The truth: You have an innate intelligence and have something important to offer the world.***

**I'm not creative** – We don't have to be painters, musicians or writers to be creative, but that is what many of us believe. If we believe we are not creative, we probably won't endeavour to explore our talents and abilities. Instead, we will live restricted lives where we never tap into our true potential. We are all infinitely creative beings, and we can be creative in our thoughts, daily tasks and routines, our words, the way we live, business ideas, activities and relationships. Creativity is inspiration followed through with action. When we realise we are infinitely creative, our lives become a work of art.

***The truth: You are innately and infinitely creative.***

For some, the shame of not being enough and feeling inferior is so painful, that the belief gets repressed and is masked by an over-inflated ego to compensate, creating narcissistic beliefs:

**I am more important than others** – the opposite of the belief "I'm not important", this lie also comes from believing we are not enough because we are expecting other people to make us feel enough. By making others inferior, the ego feels superior, with an attitude of entitlement, a pattern of treating others poorly and inevitably creating disappointment when life doesn't go our way.

***The truth: You are important … and so is everybody else.***

**Others should do as I demand** – rather than seeing others as equal beings with their own unique life path; we see other people as an extension of ourselves who are solely there as a means to getting what we want. We objectify and hold little empathy for them, and get angry when they don't deliver. The consequences of this lie will be poor and dysfunctional relationships and people leaving us.

***The truth: The more you respect and empathise with others, the more respect and empathy you will receive in return.***

**I am entitled to special treatment** – if we believe this, we become angry and disagreeable if we do not receive the treatment and reactions that we want, because "ordinary" treatment reminds us of our true core belief that we are not enough. Empty on the inside, we can only feel whole when receiving the message that we are "special".

***The truth: If you are wanting special treatment from others, learn to give it to yourself and others first.***

## Balance

Taken to their extremes, any of the above beliefs will lead to a serious imbalance in our lives, showing up as unhappiness, stress, scarcity and/or mental and physical illnesses. The knowledge that we are enough is based on a humble and balanced love and respect for ourselves that believes:

- I am worthy and deserving, but not selfish
- I give to myself and then I give to others
- I feel important but not arrogant
- I love myself and I love others
- I enjoy being alone and I enjoy feeling connected
- I speak my truth and I listen to others' truths
- I am free to come and go, and so are others
- I can fail and I can succeed

- I can work hard and I can relax and enjoy life
- I do my best and I don't have to be perfect.

## Shame

Believing we are not enough creates the emotion of shame. Holding shame, we put on a "front", believing that if others found out who we really are, we would be rejected, and the greatest human fear is the fear of rejection. This is a primal fear - being loved and accepted as a baby was tantamount to our survival. We can deny our shame and pretend it is not there, but like anything we deny, it stays in our energy field. The very energy of shame attracts to us people who treat us like we are not enough, and situations where we are shown we are not enough. Shame bleeds into every choice we make and every area of our life. It is time to shine the light on our shame, to bring it out of the dark corners and see it for the lie that it really is.

***"No one can make you feel inferior without your approval"
– Eleanor Roosevelt***

## Ancestral Shame

While some of us have experienced very painful childhoods, most of us have known a combination of love and pain. It doesn't always take a major trauma to absorb the lie that we are not enough. If we believe we are not enough, our parents believed the same lie about themselves, as did theirs and those before them. For generations we have been asleep, unaware that the challenges we face in our lives are in fact the very path we are meant to embrace in order to realise our greatness. Instead, we see our challenges as evidence that we are faulty and not enough. Children take on their parents' lies. We learn from our parents not just by what they say; we absorb their energy on all levels. Just as we inherit our genes, we inherit the lie. But there are no accidents! On a soul level, we chose our parents and all the experiences and lessons that would come from being their child. We chose this for our soul's growth and evolution.

## Forgiving our parents/caregivers

It can be very difficult to forgive key people in our lives who gave us the message that we were not enough, but these were just projections of how they felt about themselves, for they received the same messages from their parents. The day we truly grow up and become whole is the day we stop seeing our parents or caregivers as parents or caregivers, but as human beings who were conditioned with self-limiting beliefs. It wasn't their fault. We must let go of this idea of fault and blame. We are fortunate to be living in a time with a growing awareness that we have the power to transcend this conditioning, but our parents may not have been exposed to this awakened knowledge, nor capable of integrating it.

If we are still holding onto resentment and blame towards them, it is a sure sign that we are still believing we are not enough, because we are handing our power over to the person or people who unconsciously hurt us. If we believe we cannot forgive them, it is because we don't believe we have the power and resources within ourselves to overcome the hurt and shame we feel. When we choose to forgive, we are choosing to believe that we are enough, regardless of the challenges and so-called "wrongdoings" in our lives, and we can choose to be whole and healed and move on to the new.

Forgiveness cannot be forced. We simply have to be *willing* to forgive. The energy of "willing" is not forceful or contrived, but voluntary and honest. When we are willing to forgive, we can declare "I am willing to forgive those who denied me my good". This is all we need to do to set in motion an energy shift that will bring about the outcome.

One of the saddest stores I have heard was from my client Jo-Anne, who was one of seven children in an impoverished family. All of them endured physical and sexual abuse from their father while their mother slowly drank herself to death. Two of her brothers committed suicide in adulthood. Louise's life had been difficult and she struggled with shame and low self-worth. She had "tried to forgive" her parents in the past but couldn't. We spent many sessions together processing the grief and anger she felt, and at the end of every session I would ask her to declare "I am willing to forgive". In time, her face began to look different – softer – and every time I saw her there was more light in her eyes. One day she turned up for our session and said "I know this is my last session, because when I think of my parents, I no longer feel hurt or angry. I woke up this morning and felt profoundly sorry for them. They made our lives hell, but their lives had been hell to begin with."

Forgiving our family of origin is the key to healing all our relationships.

## No damage is irreversible

If we believe that the traumas in our lives are too great to overcome, they will be. If we believe that we are capable of transcending anything, then we will be able to do that, and not only that. When we transcend these wounds, we are able to help others transcend theirs, because we are living proof it is possible.

## Self-forgiveness

We are here to master the human experience. Life is a school and we are here to learn. We learn mostly by trial and error. That means we are going to make poor choices at times. But every mistake you have made in your life up until now was inevitable! With the knowledge you had at the time, of course you were going to do what you did, so there is no point blaming or punishing yourself. Mistakes are okay, as long as we learn the important lessons they present to us, atone for our errors if possible, and forgive ourselves. When the lesson has been learned, we take that valuable lesson into our future and make better choices. There is no point holding onto guilt, shame or self-hatred over past mistakes. The only person whose life will be affected will be our own – unconsciously punishing or denying ourselves over and over again.

## We are all doing the best we can

When we accept that on the human level, none of us is perfect – we are all somewhere on the path of evolution and where we are right now is where we are meant to be – then we can accept ourselves and all our faults, and we can accept others and their faults too. The past has been and gone – it no longer exists. Right here, right now, you can have a fresh slate to draw upon, but you can only have it if you let go of the guilt and shame you are holding from yesterday.

## Criticism

None of us likes to be criticised. To the extent that we believe we are not enough, we will receive criticism and it will feel like a knife being driven into us. However, not all criticism is ill-intentioned, and sometimes someone else's objective insights can be helpful. Some people (but not all) are attempting to help us by giving us constructive criticism, but if we are full of shame, we shut down and take it as evidence of our being not enough, even if the criticism is coming from someone we like and respect. If you receive criticism from someone you like and respect and find yourself shutting down, imagine a screen between you and the other person, and through that screen you allow only helpful information to filter through. The rest of it stays on the other side of the screen with the other person! If you receive criticism from someone you don't like or respect, don't take it on, because the person is not in alignment with you.

**You are not only enough; you are perfect in all your human faultiness**

If you weren't enough, you wouldn't be here. You are an important part of the Divine Universal plan. Spiritually we are all perfect, divine beings. We have all incarnated as faulty humans so as to experience and learn from Life and advance our souls. We are continually being shown what our next lesson is and in what area we are needing to grow. This is all a part of the quest of finding out who we really are – our True Self.

When we start to know we are enough, our life begins to flow in a positive, fulfilling way. We make choices out of love, not fear, and we begin to attract to us people and situations that reflect back to us our divine worth. We know we are worthy of happiness, loving relationships, abundance and personal success. We begin to see that just because someone treats us badly, it is not evidence that we are not enough. It is evidence of our wounding. We no longer need to take it personally. We lose the fear of being hurt because nothing can hurt us except our own limiting beliefs about ourselves. When we know that we are enough, we can see that everyone else is enough too. Our ability to love expands! Knowing we are enough is an inside job. It has to start within us. When the love and approval inside of us becomes greater than the outside reflections, our lives transform in wondrous ways.

**The Paradox**

We must be willing to grow and expand and to become more, and at the same time know that in this very moment we are enough.

**To be aware of:**

Become aware when you are feeling that you are not enough. You may be surprised just how often this belief is playing itself out in your life. It may start with a feeling or a thought you have about yourself or a comment from another person or an event or situation. Notice the feelings that come up. Become aware of any self-criticism or non-loving thoughts towards yourself. No other person, event or situation can make you feel this way. Only you can make yourself feel this way. The person, event or situation is showing up in your life to reflect back to you the lie you hold about yourself. Remind yourself that you are enough, even in all your human faultiness. Can you find a thought or belief that has triggered you? Refer to the common beliefs at the beginning of this chapter. Can you turn the thought or belief around to a thought or belief that is in alignment with your True Self? This will be a loving and compassionate thought that gives you a feeling of wholeness and relief. Allow yourself to move out of the vibration of fear and into the vibration of love.

**Affirmations**

I release and let go of the lie that I am not enough.

In each and every moment I am enough.

If someone treats me badly, it is not a reflection of who I am; it is a reflection of my wound.

I now no longer take others' poor treatment of me personally.

I am good enough.

I am worthy and deserving of all that my heart desires.

By giving to myself first, I am better able to give to others.

I am an important part of the Universal whole.

I am always loved and supported by the Universe.

Doing my best is good enough.

Failure is a normal part of the journey.

I am uniquely intelligent and creative and I have something to offer the world.

I am loving and lovable.

I am not only enough, I am perfect in all my human faultiness.

I choose to accept constructive criticism if it feels true.

I am willing to expand and grow and I am capable of positive change.

I love myself just the way I am.

I speak my truth with love.

I am willing to forgive those who denied me my good.

I am willing to forgive myself.

I am willing to accept others just the way they are.

I am willing to understand and empathise.

I love and approve of myself completely and unconditionally.

# LIE NUMBER FIVE

## LOVE HURTS

### The Truth:

### Love heals everything

***We are here to learn about love – what love is, and what love is not. As we come to know love and be love, we heal ourselves and our lives.***

When distilled down, there are only two vibrations in the world – love and fear. Our lives are a constant lesson about love. We are here to learn how to expand in love, and let go of fear. Both vibrations are powerful creators. The more we are in the vibration of love, the more we attract to us people who are also in this vibration. When we relate from the vibration of love, we heal our relationships, and when we relate from the vibration of fear, relationships become challenging, because wherever we hold fear, we are blocking love. The two cannot exist together.

Love is a powerful vibration that heals everything. It is the key to healing whatever is not working in our lives, but many of us confuse fear with love. Our ego mind can trick us into thinking that certain beliefs, thoughts and actions are loving when in truth, they are not. If you do not believe me, look back on your past mistakes. Were your decisions made out of love or fear? If the answer is love, ask yourself, "Was it really love? Or was it my ego mind convincing me that I was acting out of love?" The ego mind is a trickster when it comes to love.

It is only through experiencing what love is not, that we get the opportunity to clear the lies we believe about love. While we may learn early on that love is kind and compassionate, and that it isn't hate nor violence, we must also learn the finer lessons about love. Darkness descends upon our lives when we mistake love for one of love's impostors. These impostors, created by the ego mind, lead us on a loveless and unfulfilling path. Many of us have experienced painful lessons in love – in close relationships, or in a scarcity of loving relationships – as well as in our work, our homes and our everyday routines. Love is a vibration that must exist in every area of our lives if we are to reach our full potential and know true happiness. When we embrace and learn the painful lessons of what love is not, we have a greater understanding of what love is. With every lesson, we let go of an illusion and see love more clearly. If we continue to believe in an impostor to love, the pain in our life becomes greater and we go further into the darkness.

## The ten impostors to love

We have all learned lies about love. These are love's impostors. If we believe in any of these impostors, they will show up in our lives as painful challenges. Love is a pure vibration in and of itself. We taint love when we associate or confuse it with any of these impostors, which are all fear-based. Below are the ten most common impostors to love, followed by the truth about love.

**Power and control** – when we seek to control another or have power over another – "I need you to be/act this way and then I'll feel loved" - we are acting out of fear and not honouring the other person's freedom. We therefore disempower them from living their truth. Conversely, if we allow another person to have power and control over us, we are also in the vibration of fear and not honouring our own freedom.

***The truth: Love is empowering ourselves and living in freedom, and allowing others to do the same.***

**Sacrifice** – sacrificing ourselves for others has been honored for millennia. There is no positive outcome ultimately for being a martyr and putting ourselves last. How much can we be of true service if we are depleting ourselves? When we prioritise our own needs, we re-energise ourselves, enabling us to give to others in a more empowered and loving way, and we give them permission also to put themselves first.

***The truth: Love is putting ourselves first; and then giving to others.***

**Caretaking and pleasing** – looking after other people who can look after themselves and giving to others to either please them or control them creates dependency and does not enable others to live empowered lives. People who like to care-take and please are looking for their sense of self-worth from others. Taken to the extreme, caretaking and pleasing becomes an act of selfishness.

***The truth: Love is looking after ourselves, and allowing others to do the same unless it is truly needed.***

**Dependence** – overly relying on someone else can be confused with love. Wanting someone to depend on us or depending upon another is a form of control, and stunts our personal growth and prevents us from knowing our personal power and reaching our full potential. In close relationships there are going to be times when we or someone we love is going to depend on us, and we them - such as times of illness, grief, and challenges, but overly-relying on someone on a day-to-day basis does not come from a place of love, but from a place of fear. Truly loving relationships are interdependent – with a synergy of both independence and deep connection.

***The truth: Love allows individual freedom as well as deep connection.***

**Rescuing** – unless it is a real emergency, the only person we can rescue is ourselves. Rescuers tend to be victims who identify strongly with other victims. They find it difficult to see others as empowered beings who are capable of fixing their own problems. Their self-worth comes from feeling like a hero.

***The truth: Love is rescuing ourselves, and allowing others to rescue themselves unless there is an emergency.***

**Guilt** – guilt has nothing to do with love, and yet many of us confuse this emotion with love. If we are acting out of guilt, we are acting out of a deep sense of inadequacy or shame within ourselves and are driven by the thoughts "I have to" and "I should" rather than "I would love to". Guilt-ridden people also project their guilt onto others with expectations of "you have to" and "you should".

***The truth: Love's actions come from a sense of love and genuine desire.***

**Idolisation and charm** - placing people, things and concepts on a pedestal will inevitably lead to disappointment when the reality of the person, thing or concept shows itself fully. Charming words can be music to our ears, but they are driven by manipulation, which is fear-based. To the extent which we have a *need* for love, we will hold a weakness for idolisation and charm or weave a spell on others with our charm.

***The truth: Love allows us to see, hear and relate to others in an honest and realistic way.***

**Addiction** - the extreme emotional state of infatuation is often mistaken for "love". When it wears off (and it inevitably does), we plummet into disappointment and want the "high" feelings we first experienced to return, because we don't have enough love within ourselves to either sustain a more realistic relationship or to walk away because we have realised we were blinded by a lie.

***The truth: Love is found from within first, and is consistent and grounded.***

**Perfection** – believing that we or others must be perfect in order to be loved or lovable will ensure we will experience disappointment in love. The more we can love the "faulty" parts of ourselves, the more we can love the faulty parts of others.

***The truth: Love sees beyond faults.***

**Narcissism** – taking the concept of self-love to the extreme, narcissism manifests as extreme self-centredness with a disregard for others. Genuine self-love manifests as loving ourselves first, so as to love and give to others.

***The truth: Love is loving and honouring ourselves first and then loving and honouring others.***

## The need for love

The need for love is different to the desire for love. Desire says "I would like love". Need says "I have to have love". The impostors come from a sense of neediness, borne from emptiness, created by the fearful ego mind. The need for love actually pushes real love away. Emptiness attracts emptiness. When we begin to connect with our True Self, we become full of love, and this fullness attracts fullness.

## The lesson in love is always about you

If there is anyone in your life with whom you are experiencing difficulties, they are here to reflect back to you where you are withholding love from them and yourself. Your ego mind will make it all about the other person and attempt to blame them, but from this perspective there is no personal growth for you. If there are any situations in your life that are challenging you right now, they are also here to show you where you are withholding love – from yourself and/or others – and are a healing opportunity for you to become a greater expression of love.

## Conditional love creates shame

From the moment we are born, we are learning about love. Our lives are a kaleidoscope of experiences, some loving and some not, and on the journey of life we develop core beliefs about love that guide our choices and create our life path. As we grew up, most of us learned that love was conditional. We would be loved if we were well-behaved children, if we shared, achieved well at school and displayed good manners. Already we were learning that the love we received from our parents was limited, so we developed strategies to earn love.

Most of us learned that we could only express certain parts of ourselves in order to be loved, and that we must hide the "unacceptable" parts such as anger, jealousy and sexuality. These "negative" feelings were shoved into the shadows, and not allowed any light, and we in turn took on a deep belief that we were innately bad and guilty, because if we were "good", we wouldn't feel this way. This became our mantel of shame that we would take with us into our future, unaware that in every human being there is everything – both the dark and the light - and if we shone the light of love on these hidden parts of ourselves and owned it all, we could let go of our shame.

***"There is a little bit of Hitler in all of us"***
***– Elizabeth Kubler-Ross***

Instead we denied and hid these parts of ourselves, and thought we could rid ourselves of them by pretending they weren't there, but what we disown in ourselves we project onto other people, disliking them and judging them for displaying the parts of ourselves we have disowned. These hidden parts of ourselves create the very challenges we need so as to transcend them – difficult people, negative events, hardship, scarcity and "bad luck"- show up in our lives. They are our karma, created by our own shame.

**Self-love**

Love must begin with ourselves. Our relationship with ourselves must be given priority over others – whether it be our partner, parents, friends, children or anyone else. Many of us were not taught or shown this, and so we deny ourselves love and nurturing, while putting others' needs before our own. We then become drained by our relationships. Our level of self-love will be reflected back to us by the relationships we manifest. If we are in an unloving partnership, our partner will reflect back to us our belief in our "un-lovability". If we feel lonely or disconnected, it is a reflection of our lack of connection within.

A lack of self-love will show itself as self-judgment, self-criticism and self-hatred. We must transform our relationship with ourselves in order to create more loving relationships in our lives, and this begins with kindness and compassion towards ourselves. Become aware of your inner voice. Is it kind and nurturing, or is it critical and blaming? Stay aware of your inner dialogue and make it your highest priority to change it to a loving, kind and accepting one. We must all learn to be our own loving best friend.

## Body Image

The relationship you have with your body is indicative of the relationship you have with your inner being. Many people struggle to love their bodies. The ugliness that is present on the inside begins to show on the outside. It is not unusual for people who have experienced sexual abuse to gain weight, effectively protecting themselves from further harm. Unexpressed anger or self-hatred can show itself as acne and hyper-sensitivity may manifest as skin disorders. If we choose to become hard and bitter about our life experiences to date, it will eventually show on our face. Our inner beliefs become manifest on the outside, creating further self-hatred. If we have any issues around our physical attractiveness, diet and exercise may work temporarily, but we must be willing to go deeper if we wish to truly heal, and self-love is the key.

## Loneliness

The ego is not connected to the Source, and so it feels profoundly alone. Not surprisingly, it craves outside attachments to avoid the emptiness it fears the most – loneliness. This fear of being alone can keep us in relationships and situations that are no longer good for us. Our True Self, connected to the Divine Source, knows that the emptiness – the space, the void, or whatever we wish to call it – is actually the field of all possibilities, and there is nothing to fear and everything to embrace in this space. If we are experiencing situations where we find ourselves alone and feeling lonely, it is an invitation from the Universe to re-connect with our True Selves. This is where we will find true love, and from there we will manifest it in our lives. If ever you find yourself feeling lonely, sit with the feeling. Allow yourself to feel it. Beneath the feeling of loneliness will be sadness. Sit with whatever comes up. Do not fear the feelings. The more you do this, the more you connect with yourself and face what you fear. Do not rush to fill in the space.

## Romantic relationships

Most of us want a partner who will love us unconditionally, and yet we struggle to love them unconditionally. We long for the ideal parent we never had. We have learned that romantic love is a double-edged sword – when we fall in love, we feel whole and healed, until our old wounds get opened up and love gets wiped out by fear.

We have been conditioned to believe that love is a commodity that can only be found outside of ourselves and that someone else's love is going to heal us. In any romantic relationship, when the high of infatuation wears off, the rose-coloured glasses fall off too. We discover that our knight in shining armour is an ordinary man with his own personal struggles and flaws, and the Goddess has her imperfections, and so many of us feel disappointed by romantic love. Our ego thinks "this isn't what I signed up for!"

As we acquire our battle scars in romantic love, we begin to believe that it's not safe to love and that love hurts. So we fear love, withdrawing our love and creating a protective shell around ourselves. But it wasn't love that hurt us; it was our misperception of what love is that hurt us. Love doesn't wound; it can only heal.

Many of us have overlaid love with other expectations – the impostors. The child within us yearns to be in a state of bliss, feeling nurtured, valued and safe. We want our partner, who is also yearning for this state of bliss, to repair us, but only we can repair ourselves. Our partner is in our life to reflect back to us where we are withholding love from ourselves, and we are in theirs for the same reason. If we remain aware and inquisitive about the reactions we have to our partner, and are willing to own our wounds, the romantic relationship is an intensive lesson as to what love is and what love is not. It is the relationship and its lessons that heals us; not our partner.

**Every relationship we have is a reflection of our capacity to love**

If you have experienced a toxic relationship, that person has come to show you where you yourself are holding a toxin. Your ego mind will tell you that the other person is bad or wrong and you are good, and right, but this is not true. The concepts of "good/bad" and" right/wrong" are from the ego mind and have no place in any relationship. The wound in the other person has come into your life to show you the wound in you. Remember, the lesson is always about you. It is not for you to judge the other person. Judging the other person is the ego's way of taking your attention away from what it is you are meant to be learning. As soon as you are judging, you have fallen into ego.

If someone has bullied you, they are showing you your wound of feeling powerless; if you attract angry people, these people are reflecting back to you the anger within yourself; if someone has left you, they are showing you your belief and fear of abandonment; if someone constantly criticises you, they are showing you your lack of self-approval. No challenge to love can appear in your life unless the challenge already exists within you. When we heal the blocks to love within ourselves, the outside challenges begin to fall away. If you are experiencing a difficult relationship, a key question to ask yourself is:

*"What is it in me that is blocking love?"*

## Seek to understand, not judge

If we are judging anyone, we will be blocking love from them. To truly love anyone, we must first seek to understand them. The ego mind believes that we can only feel love for those who agree with us and who treat us well, and that we cannot love those who disagree with us or do not treat us the way we would like to be treated. This is a lie. Seeking to understand another does not mean that we must analyse them microscopically; nor does it mean that we will ever achieve a complete understanding; it simply means that we hold the intention to remain open to their truth, knowing that others may see the world through a different lens than we do, and that their perspective is not "wrong" – it is simply different to ours. If we find ourselves judging someone, we must ask ourselves:

*"What is it in me that needs to judge this person?"*

This attitude takes compassion and kindness. We are all the sum total of our experiences and acquired beliefs up until this moment, and everyone is doing the best they know how, even a person who is treating you poorly. We must let go of the ego mind's illusion of how a relationship is supposed to be, and allow the relationship to be what it is going to be.

We can accept that we may never fully understand another human being with whom we experience difficulty or that the person operates from a different paradigm than we do, and we don't need to take that difference personally. This allows us to remain in the vibration of love with that person – loving them and ourselves unconditionally. Of course this does not mean that we stay in close relationships that are abusive, neglectful or that do not serve us. The love for ourselves must always come first, so that we can live full and loving lives. We are too valuable a being to share our lives on a day-to-day basis with those who persistently blame, abuse or neglect us. However, just because we have chosen not to be with a person doesn't mean we cannot love them; it is in our highest good to do just that.

So many of us have felt challenged to love a parent, an ex-partner or someone who has hurt us. Loving them will remain impossible unless we are willing to understand them. When we choose to know another's story, starting with their childhood and the wounds they gathered, we no longer need to take their treatment of us personally because we realise that they were operating from the lies they came to believe and we can have compassion for them (without necessarily inviting them back into our lives).

## Love creates boundaries

Setting a boundary means refusing to compromise on our personal standards and values which are important to us. By setting boundaries, we are honouring ourselves. Some of us were not shown how to set boundaries when we were young, and so do not understand the importance of them. We must love ourselves enough to put our own wellbeing first and creating boundaries supports us in staying true to ourselves and our values, and from becoming energetically drained by others. Having healthy boundaries in all our relationships is an act of love, even with those we are closest to.

Many of us have grown up believing that love means collapsing our personal boundaries. Our boundaries will differ in various relationships, for example the boundaries you set with your spouse will be more open and relaxed than the boundaries you set with a work colleague. Boundaries do not have to be concrete walls; they can be flexible depending on the situation and circumstance. Creating healthy boundaries with anyone who has hurt us in the past protects us from further harm, so that we may remain in the vibration of love with them. Sometimes love has to say "No", "That is enough" and "I'm not comfortable and I need to leave".

### The wounded child

Whenever we feel a strong negative reaction – one that seems out of proportion to what is actually happening – it is because a childhood wound has been triggered. We all have a wounded child. The more we become aware of it, the more able we are to self-soothe. If you experience a strong reaction, feel the feelings and then imagine within you the little child who is hurting. Imagine soothing this little child and telling them that she/he is loved and you are there for them. You can be the ideal loving parent to your own inner child.

## Loving our children

The relationships we have with our children are a reflection of the relationship we have with our own inner child. The inner child is the part of you that is still a child – this child can be light-hearted, innocent, playful and free. It can also be deeply wounded. Whatever childhood wounds are buried within us that have not been healed, will be inherited by our children. If we keep them repressed, our children will carry the imprints and very often act them out. Unaware of our own repressions, we may label our child as difficult or troubled. If we are in judgment of our kids, we block our love to them. Some well-intentioned parents will take their child to a professional for help, unaware that the person who needs to heal is actually themselves. I was one of those parents! When parents begin their own healing journey, a miracle often unfolds– their children begin to heal.

If we have ignored our wounded inner child, we will be holding blocks to love, and our parenting behaviours will be out of balance, reflecting this. We will either give too much or too little, and these actions will not be coming from the vibration of love, but from an impostor. The parents who want to give too much to their children - giving them the things they didn't have when they were young, in an attempt to heal the sense of scarcity that exists within their own inner child – will eventually be shown that over-compensation is not love. If we shower them with material things, it is likely because we felt deprived in this way as a child, or we feel guilty that we are not loving them enough in more meaningful ways, such as giving them our time and truly listening to them. Our children become the proverbial "spoilt children" because we taught them a lie about love.

Some of us believe that we must sacrifice for our children. My client Laura came to see me because she felt drained and worn out from giving to her family. I recognised my old self in her immediately. For many years I had held the belief that my children must come first above everything. I believed this because my own wounded child felt that she wasn't a priority when she was young, and so I sought to make my children's lives better by over-functioning for them. Laura was drained emotionally, physically and financially. She worried constantly about her children's problems and felt she didn't have a life because most of her time was taken driving her children to their many activities, helping them with their school work, projects, sporting activities and social lives and trying to fix their problems. She and her husband were feeling financial strain as well, because they felt obligated to send their kids to the "best" private schools available. This came from the belief that their children would be disadvantaged if they were not given every possible opportunity.

"Have you considered that your children will be disadvantaged if you do send them to the expensive private school?" I asked. "They will feel the financial stress in the family, and also feel pressure to perform because of the sacrifice you are making for them".

Choices made out of sacrifice never ultimately serve anyone. Laura chose to let go of the belief that she must sacrifice her own happiness and financial freedom for her children, and from this choice she and her husband chose to send their children to schools that were more affordable. She also chose to start giving to herself more and to cut down on the number of extra-curricular activities the children undertook, and found that the balance and inner peace this created within her had a powerful healing effect upon the whole family.

Some parents are ambitious for their children. If we believe our children must excel at school or a certain activity, it may be because we felt we weren't good enough when we were kids or that we didn't have enough opportunities, or we are unconsciously re-enacting our parents' pattern. Our childhood wounds are channelled into dreams for our child, wanting them to live up to an ideal that has nothing to do with who our child is and what they truly desire. The child feels pressured and controlled by parents who are unaware as to why they are projecting their own dormant dreams onto them. Some adults literally live their lives through their children, believing this is love, but love respects and honours others as separate, unique beings.

Parents who give too little on the other hand, wrapped up in their own lives and ambitions and believing in a scarcity of time, may resent their children, and also feel guilty. Resentment and guilt do not allow any room for love.

Parenting requires a balance – of giving to self and giving to our children. Research has shown that the most common regret of the dying is not having invested enough time and love in their family relationships, particularly in their relationships with their children.

Love deeply engages and also allows space for a child to explore who they are. While we may guide a child, love does not attempt to control a child. Our children may be born from us, but they each have incarnated for their own unique reasons and purpose. With the rate of change that is happening on earth, we cannot even begin to imagine what their adult world will look like. As parents, we are here to do the best we can (but not at cost to self), to love and encourage them to be true to themselves, and surrender the outcome.

Some children are more challenging than others – strong-willed, restless, sensitive, individualistic or rebellious, and often diagnosed with disorders. Rather than see our "difficult" children as an affliction that is ruining our lives, it is time to see the truth – they are our healing angels who are here to open our hearts and show us where we are withholding love. On a soul level, the child made an agreement with us – to give us a fast-track lesson to knowing unconditional love!

Many of the children being born now are a higher vibration than us, and see the world in a very different way than we do. They find it difficult to fit into the present structures such as the current schooling model. Not surprisingly, we may find it difficult to understand them. No amount of rules, threats or ultimatums work as an effective parenting or teaching tool. The only way to mend the bridge is to love them unconditionally, and allow them to be who they are. This does not mean that we do not provide structure and natural consequences, but these measures will fail to help a child unless they are provided within a framework of unconditional love.

## Become aware of your heart chakra

The heart chakra is located at the centre of the chest and is the energy centre of love, compassion and forgiveness. By feeling into the heart chakra every day and consciously breathing in and out of this area, you can begin to open your heart more. Become aware of how you feel in this area. When the heart is open, you feel light and joyful. When it is closed, you feel heavy and joyless. By consciously opening the heart chakra, you can allow love to flow and then life begins to flow. If you wish to relate in a more loving way, consciously open your heart to the other person. If you are finding it difficult to relate to someone, remain aware of what is happening to your heart chakra throughout the interaction, and be willing to keep your heart open. If you are experiencing difficulty, ask yourself:

*"What would love do now?"*

## You are love

Love is the core of our very nature. We don't become more loving beings by "adding" anything to ourselves. Rather, we become more loving beings by "taking away" the misperceptions of the ego mind. That's when we realise that love was there all along, and the more we recognise and honour love, the more blissful our lives become. We discover that love is not just a feeling, a thought, an action or something that is given or received. We discover that we *are* love.

It is only from making mistakes about love and learning the lessons from the impostors to love that we can expand our truth of what love is. Rather than seeing love's impostors as untruths that led to bad choices, we can choose to see them as lessons along our path that showed us the way to love, and we are all on the path to ever greater love. In every moment, you have a choice to either be in love or in fear, and the choice you make is the difference between living in Heaven or in hell. When we begin to open our hearts and to choose thoughts and actions in the vibration of love, we enter a parallel Universe – a shift to bliss.

## The Paradox

Every human being wants to be loved by another, yet the only way to create love in our lives is to find love within.

## To be aware of:

Whenever you feel at ease and at peace, you are in the vibration of love. When you are feeling stressed, anxious, angry or any other "negative" emotion, you have dropped out of the vibration of love and into the vibration of fear. Your centre of love is your heart chakra, located in the centre of your chest. It is the gateway to your soul. Staying aware of how you are feeling in this area is an accurate barometer of your current vibration. When you are in the vibration of love, your heart chakra feels light, open and free. When you are in fear, you will feel a closed, heavy or tight sensation in the heart area.

There is no point in trying to push negative feelings away. Instead, acknowledge the feeling and stay aware of the physical sensations in the heart. Close your eyes and feel the sensation, while breathing in and out of your heart. Ask your heart if there is something it wants to tell you – you may get an answer or you may not. The important thing is that you are listening to your heart. With every breath in and out, hold the intention to then relax, open and expand your heart chakra, allowing love to fill your entire being.

## Affirmations

I choose love over fear.

I am open and willing to love more.

I am willing to know what love is.

I am willing to release old wounds that are creating shame.

I am willing to release old wounds that are blocking love.

Love is freedom for myself and others.

I release and let go of the need for love, and choose instead to desire love.

The most important relationship I have is the relationship with myself.

I am willing to nurture and heal my inner child.

I speak to myself with kindness and compassion.

I choose to be my own best friend.

The loving relationship I have with myself extends out to others.

I look beyond my faults and the faults of others.

I now release the need to judge others.

I seek to understand others.

I speak to others with kindness and compassion.

I accept that others may view the world differently to me.

I love and accept others just the way they are.

I choose to be honest and realistic.

I maintain healthy boundaries in all my relationships.

I am willing to open my heart.

I am love.

# LIE NUMBER SIX

## IT'S NOT SAFE TO CHANGE

### The Truth:

### Staying the same will become unbearable

***Embrace change as it is essential to the flow of life, and to your growth and ultimate happiness. If you do not embrace change, pain and dissatisfaction will build up in your life until you reach a tipping point and are forced to surrender to change.***

Every challenge we encounter is pushing us to transform, and holds the key to the next step of our life's transformational journey. Most of us fear change. Some fear it to such an extent that they live their lives in a straightjacket, fearful of stepping outside of their proverbial "comfort zone". Most "comfortable" lives are asleep with lies. Until we begin the journey of awakening, we may not be aware of just how many unspoken rules and self-inflicted restrictions exist within us, limiting our vision and potential.

From the outer beliefs in traditions to the unspoken hidden beliefs handed down through the generations, we live like goldfish in bowls, unaware that there is an ocean to swim in. Wherever we feel stuck, blaming others or situations, or stating the words "I have to" or "I should" will be an indication of where we are blocking our personal growth process. The fearful ego mind blocks us from knowing that in each and every moment we have choice. Resisting transformation may feel safe, but our soul yearns for something more.

As the earth energies change and we awaken, the need for internal transformation will become stronger, and we may begin to feel discontent with our current circumstances. People with whom we once resonated no longer interest us; the things that once gave us satisfaction now seem meaningless; a sense of injustice may become stronger. A restlessness may enter our being and we may feel the urge to live more congruently with our own truth. At the same time we fear making the changes that it would require of us. There may be times when we feel that it would be so much easier to go back to our old unawakened self, but alas, we cannot, because to go back feels like a death.

Change is inevitable, and unless we embrace it and go with it, we will become "stuck" in a state of dissatisfaction. Sometimes in these circumstances, the Universe may force change upon us in a sudden and unexpected way– an illness, a partner leaving, a crisis, an accident or other unforeseen circumstance.

A crisis is a storm that has been building for years – a culmination of opportunities for change that have been ignored or not dealt with over a period of time. If we don't want to face major crises, we must learn to make changes proactively and willingly throughout our lives, rather than waiting for a crisis to throw us into a new vibration.

At age 45 I experienced a sudden and unexpected mid-life crisis that threw me and my family into turmoil. It was only in hindsight that I could see how this storm had been brewing for years. I had suppressed my own needs for freedom, love and expression for a long time, believing that putting others before myself was what I was here to do. The Universe had other plans for me.

### Be the change you want to see in the world

There are many good people in the world who have good intentions, however those intentions mean nothing without action. Instead of lamenting, criticising and theorising about the change we would like for ourselves, our communities, our countries and the earth, we must take action that supports the change we desire. The Universe loves action. Many people don't take action because they think "What's the use? It won't get me anywhere." This thought is attached to an outcome. When we take action, we must hold onto an intention, but detach from the outcome.

Every action we take creates an energy wave towards our desired outcome. If we are not sure what action we need to take, we must surrender our intention to the Source and ask for signs and guidance for what we need to do. Our course of action will make itself known in divine timing.

## Fear of change

If we fear change, it is because we fear losing something. Fear is a normal part of the human experience. The level of fear in us has a direct correlation to how great a hold the ego mind has over us. The more aware we are of our fear and acknowledge it, the less power we give to the ego mind. If we are faced with difficult circumstances or decisions that are bringing up fear, we must ask ourselves:

*What is the worst that can happen?*

By examining the worst possible scenario, we face our fear. Many people are too frightened to ask this question. The ego's instinct is to push fear away, and pretend it's not there, but the only way to transcend fear is to own it, accept it and feel it. Deepening into whatever feelings come up for us is how we face and transcend fear. This is true courage. Fear will continue to cripple us until we realise that we are fuelling fear's power by avoiding it.

**"Life shrinks or expands**
**in proportion to one's courage"**
**– Anais Nin**

## Fear of the unknown

We do not believe possible what we have not yet experienced, and so we cling to the known, resisting the insecurity of not knowing what is next. We want to believe that life offers us lasting guarantees, and yet life has a way of showing us that there are none. The problem with not moving out into the unknown, is that we become bored of life because there is no risk, no adventure and no aliveness, and in this place we wither. Our True Self wants to be challenged and to grow. The True Self knows that the unknown is the field of all possibilities.

## Fear of letting go

There is no way that anything new or exciting can happen in our life unless we are willing to release the things that are no longer serving us. As we let go of old beliefs, it will follow that we will need to let go of old ways of being, and of situations or people whom we no longer resonate with. Some people may simply fade out of our life; others we may have to walk away from. Letting go can be a profoundly painful process. If we do not choose to let go, however, we will remain "stuck", unable to bring our blossoming inner truth into our outer lives, and we will not only feel unfulfilled; we will feel stagnant. Nothing can grow in stagnant energy.

When the winds of change begin to blow, there will be pain no matter what we choose. If our lives remain the same, we will feel bored, and unfulfilled. If we choose to change, the process will involve loss and uncertainty. The difference however, is that one path leads to more of the same perceived security and safety, while the other path leads to growth, personal expansion and feeling alive. There is a force underlying every life and when we allow ourselves to follow that force and not resist it, there is a beauty to the process of transformation. If we disregard that force, we take ourselves out of the Universal Flow and our lives feel blocked.

Our soul will continue to create the circumstances needed for our evolution. This may manifest as difficult relationships or circumstances, depression, conflict, illness or crisis. We have the choice to let go and follow our bliss and accept the consequences, or remain stuck in our old lives and accept the consequences. The choice is always ours.

## The consequences of change

Sometimes even small changes can feel frightening. Have you ever thought "I would love to do that" or "I would love to be like that, but":

- That would be selfish
- What would people think?
- My partner wouldn't like it

- I don't have the time
- It doesn't feel safe
- I can't afford it
- It's too late
- I'm too old.

We know that if we choose to create positive change in our lives, there will be a price to pay. Or to put it another way, there will be an energy exchange. There always is for anything that is worth having, and so it is wise to keep this in mind.

On the other hand, change is always an opportunity to grow and to smash through self-limiting beliefs. Let's take a closer look at the aforementioned beliefs:

**That would be selfish** – there is nothing wrong with doing something that you alone want to do. Selfishness is expecting others to do what you want them to do.

**What would people think?** – we have no control over what other people think, and if we allow their opinions to control our lives, we are dooming ourselves to live mediocre lives.

**My partner wouldn't like it** – partners can understandably feel threatened if we choose to change, but if the change is in our highest good, it is automatically in theirs also, even if it doesn't feel like it.

**I don't have the time** – if something is important to us, we have the ability to create the time for it.

**It doesn't feel safe** – change very often doesn't feel safe, so we must ask ourselves "What is the worst that can happen?" If the worst scenario truly is unbearable, then don't do it.

**I can't afford it** – if something is important to us, we have the ability to create the financial means for it to happen.

**It's too late** – life is one opportunity after another and rarely is it too late.

**I'm too old** – it is a belief of the mass-consciousness that at certain ages we must be in a particular stage doing particular things, but many inspiring older people in the world have shown us that we can achieve great things in the older years of our lives.

### Letting go of the fear of what other people think

We may find that we upset people when we change, especially those close to us who are not in alignment with our new vibration. They are unable to understand why we are changing, and may feel fearful or even threatened, just as we would if we were in their shoes. Some people may be outwardly hostile towards us for daring to break the unspoken rules. We may be judged as selfish, trouble-making or even crazy. Trying to explain ourselves may lead to further judgment and criticism. When we are not in the same vibration as those around us and we are being judged by them, acceptance is an act of grace. There is no point in attempting to justify ourselves or go into battle with those whose beliefs don't match ours. If there is too much of a vibrational difference, it is unlikely we will reach an understanding.

One of the greatest blocks to transformation is worrying about what other people think and wanting to be liked. Other peoples' judgments and expectations can prevent us from accessing the inner compass of our True Self. We can lose a great deal of energy trying to live up to others' expectations, all the while betraying ourselves. Most of us have been conditioned to live this way. The group mentality has dominated the way we have lived for millennia. We have needed to belong to families and tribes for protection and survival, but tribal survival is now no longer an issue. The new paradigm is requiring us to now be true to ourselves. We no longer need to belong to the tribe, because our True Self knows we belong to the Earth.

If we are making choices based on what other people think, we become slaves to those whose approval we seek. Our ego mind seeks approval, and loves admiration. It thrives on positive feedback from others, even if it isn't genuine! Many people make grave mistakes when they fall for praise or flattery. The ego mind, believing we are not enough, will lap up compliments, because there is a scarcity of inner love and acceptance within. We then become reliant on the outside feedback for our feelings of self-worth, and are vulnerable to the desires, control and manipulation of those who want us to be a certain way. We then base our decisions on how these people want us to be.

When we are true to ourselves – that is the True Self and not the ego mind - our choices and actions will automatically be not only for our highest good, but for the highest good of all. Likewise, if someone we are close to decides to be true to themselves, it is good for us, even if we cannot see how we can benefit. We must all learn to be true to ourselves first, and then be true to others, respecting that we each have the freedom to choose what we want, and that it is not in our highest good to sacrifice what we truly want so as to keep another person happy

Ed, a man in his early 60's, had been depressed for two years. I detected that he had a pattern of sacrificing his own desires so as to keep the peace in his family.

"Tell me, if you could live your ideal life, what would it look like?" I asked.

"I would buy a motorbike and get out on the weekends into the country, but my wife doesn't like motorbikes and thinks it's childish."

"What is it that riding a motorbike in the country represents to you?"

"Freedom, adventure, happiness!"

"So why not do it?"

"My wife wouldn't like it."

"But you are not your wife! Your wife is free to do the things that inspire her, and you are free to do the things that inspire you. Marriage doesn't mean you must stop growing and finding yourself. Preventing another person from living their dreams is imprisonment, not marriage."

It is not an uncommon belief that we must sacrifice parts of ourselves to satisfy our partner, in the fear we won't be loved if we are true to ourselves. Many of us have done this unconsciously – I know I did – and over time we lose ourselves. Arguing for our limitations may feel safe, but growth is about expanding, not contracting, and relationships require creating space to allow growth, as opposed to denying each other's growth.

Ed bought his motorbike, even though his wife disapproved at the time. The last time I saw Ed he looked happier and younger, and his wife was enjoying her free time pursuing her love of yoga and gardening, and sometimes she would take a trip on the motorbike with him.

Many of us fear change because we do not wish to hurt or disappoint other people, so much so that we will hurt ourselves over and over again. This is a self-inflicted tragedy. Unable to put our needs first, we eventually grow resentful, but remain clinging to life circumstances that have run their course, too fearful of judgment and letting other people down, not being liked, shunned and the uncertainty of what will follow.

## When partners want different things

It is not uncommon for long-term partners to reach a point in their relationship where they have grown apart and they both want different things. Two people face a dilemma – do we stay together and sacrifice our individual needs, or do we go our separate ways and be true to ourselves? There is no right or wrong answer to this dilemma. Some partners are able to accommodate and allow space for change and freedom, and others cannot. Sometimes there is no point in continuing the relationship, as there is not enough common ground left between the couple. If a long-term relationship or marriage ends, it is not a "failure", it has simply run its course. The two people came together to learn and grow for a period of their lives. When differences become greater than commonalities, it is a sign that their soul contract is completed.

## From judgment to compassion

If we are choosing to follow our true path and feeling fearful about it, it is inevitable that we are going to be judged and even disapproved of by some, because if we fear judgment, we will create it. Being the recipient of harsh judgment can be a humbling experience and holds valuable lessons for us – having experienced it, we are less likely to want to judge others. We know how it feels and we realise we are all on own unique journey, experiencing our necessary soul lessons. From the experience of being judged, we begin to change our own habits of judgment towards others and instead choose compassion over judgment.

Judgment is the ego's way of viewing others through eyes of fear. If we respond to judgment by feeling defensive and attempting to justify ourselves, we are also in fear and holding a belief that we are somehow wrong. Just because the outside world judges us as wrong doesn't mean we are!

## Baby steps Vs big leaps

Change can feel overwhelming when our ego mind convinces us that there are only two choices: to stay the same or choose drastic change, and so we think in extreme terms:

- Do I stay or leave my marriage?
- Do I jump from this career into something completely new?

This is how we stay stuck. The change feels so overwhelming, that we never do anything about it. So often, these are not the questions we need to be asking ourselves. Instead, we simply need to choose the next step on our transformational path:

- What can I do to become a more empowered person in my marriage?

- What steps can I take towards a new vocation that I am suited to?

Change is a process; it doesn't have to be a leap. There are no shortcuts to transformation – it is a step-by-step process and we cannot skip the steps. When we choose to take one step at a time, we face each fear one by one and we allow change to unfold in a slower, more organic way. Lots of little steps eventually lead to big change.

***"The journey of 1,000 miles***
***begins with one step."***
***– Lao Tzu***

## The loneliness of transformation

There is a universal aspect to every transformational path, and that is, at some point, we will find ourselves feeling profoundly alone. As the ego mind fears being alone, it cannot see that this is a gift from the Universe – an opportunity to explore the most important relationship that we will ever have – the relationship with ourselves. We will never truly know ourselves by adding more to our lives; we can only truly know ourselves by stripping away our outside attachments. This is where the true wealth is. If we are feeling alone, it is time to become our own best friend. We must trust in the process – and transformation is a process – and live in the now, knowing that we are safe and when the time is right, the Universe will show us the outer manifestation of our new vibration.

Between letting go of the old and bringing in the new, we can feel like we are in a strange limbo land – lost, anchorless and alone - wondering who we are and where we are. We have let go of who we thought we were, and we are not sure of who we are right now. The old identity has gone; the new identity is yet to emerge. We are the caterpillar in its cocoon, who is not yet a butterfly. No longer can we rely on the outside feedback for who we are and where we are. We are literally flying blind to Heaven knows where - and we must trust that Heaven does know where!

## Disheartenment

During the process of change, it is normal to at times feel lost and disheartened, and even hopeless, questioning whether the pain of change is really worth it. We may have let go of beliefs, situations or relationships that no longer resonate with us, and the empty space where these once existed feels like a chasm.

- I've let go of my old patterns, but nothing positive seems to be happening
- I've let go of the people in my life who put me down, but I'm lonely
- I've let go of the job that I hated, but I still haven't found the right job.

What you are experiencing today is simply the expression of what you believed yesterday. The Universe needs time to catch up! This "no man's land" is part of the transformational process, but these thoughts and feelings do not need to take over and sabotage our lives.

When we rely on our outside world as our barometer to tell us where we are at, we are relying on an unreliable instrument. While we may have raised our vibration internally, we must allow time for the external manifestation to emerge. Our challenge now is to maintain an attitude of optimism in a world of uncertainty. Just because we don't like where we are right now, doesn't mean that we are going to feel this way forever, or that we are not going to manifest a better life for ourselves.

When we feel disheartened, it is easy to allow our ego mind to take over with negative thoughts:

- I should never have left my job
- I thought I'd be better off, but I'm not
- I've made a mistake
- What was I thinking?

These thoughts effectively block the manifestation process, so we must deepen into the present moment, feel our current feelings and weed out any lies that dwell behind those feelings. We can then replace these thoughts of disheartenment with:

*"Even though I feel lost and disheartened right now, I trust in the Universe to create my life anew in divine and perfect timing."*

***"When you're going through hell, keep going!" – Winston Churchill***

## Divine timing

Everything happens in Divine timing. Our ego mind likes to think that it is in charge of the "when", but it isn't. If we are in our ego mind, we will get impatient and frustrated with the process of change, effectively blocking the Universal energies. We must surrender our ego mind's desires and expectations around timing so as to allow the Universe to do its work.

## Faith and trust

Not listening to the fearful ego mind and following the guidance of the True Self takes faith and trust – faith that the Universe is actually on our side and forever propelling us towards our highest good, and trusting that it will provide for us in whatever way it sees fit. When we have faith and trust, we embody a profound peace. We realise that every moment is perfect. We can allow everything around us to be out of control and yet we can still feel anchored, safe and secure within. This is true security.

The more we trust in the Universe, the more we know we are always safe. If we do not choose to trust in the Universe, it cannot provide for us. This is a two-way street. We trust and the Universe provides. We don't trust and the Universe does not provide. In each and every moment, we must be willing to choose trust over doubt.

## Courage

Living a life guided by the True Self in the face of a world still struggling with its ego fears takes courage. Be prepared to be told that you are not living in the real world, that you should be more concerned about your future, your career, finances, or others. You may be called a dreamer! All these are projections of the well-intentioned person's ego mind fears. Some will say that you are not seeing things realistically – and you won't be, from their point of view, because from their point of view, you need to be fearful, pessimistic and worried. We must not allow ourselves to dive into fear with the mass-consciousness, the expectations of others and by our own limited belief in ourselves. Those who are in touch with their True Selves fly in the face of convention, not to be rebellious, but simply to live their truth.

If we are going through a deep transformation, life can get seemingly worse before it gets better. Courage doesn't mean that we are fearless. Courage is acknowledging our fear and moving forward in spite of it. The more we act from the guidance of our True Self, the better the circumstances we create, and as we see these gifts begin to appear in our lives (no matter how small), our doubts begin to dissolve, fuelling us with more courage.

Blair was a lawyer. Not long into his career, he realised that he didn't enjoy it; in fact he felt stressed, unhappy and overwhelmed most of the time. He saw little evidence of what had guided him to study law in the first place, which was a strong sense of social justice. He began to suffer severe anxiety which led to a breakdown. He left the firm he was working for and sought healing, which initiated a journey of awakening. Blair became a Reiki healer and is currently studying life coaching. Guided by his True Self, he found constant Universal support along the way. Blair created his own website and social media marketing, and realised there was a need for it. He could assist others who needed his services and from this, he could financially support himself while studying. With more time available to him, he allowed space for Divine inspiration to come through, creating a series of guided Reiki meditations. Blair is on his own unique path, guided by his True Self.

## The true path to bliss

When we follow the path that excites us, that makes us feel alive, joyful and purposeful, this is our true path to bliss. Our true path is unique to us. As we listen to the wisdom of our True Self, and live its truth, the less hold the outer world has on us. No longer do we need to travel the beaten path, for we are enjoying the adventure of finding our own way. We can enjoy the world for what it is, and live our own truth within it. We no longer identify with the outer expectations and lower vibrations. The love within us has the power to transform our world. We cannot be positively transformed through any other vibration except that of love, and neither can the world around us.

We will be met by challenges, each one showing us a lie we are holding, but no challenge is ever handed to us without the means of resolving it. If we remain present and accepting of the challenge, keeping our heart open to love, we will be met by answers. Teachers, helpers, messages and signs will guide us. And as we find our way through each challenge and release the old lies held within us, we ascend further into bliss. For a time it may feel like we are pushing a boulder up a hill – it is not uncommon to be bombarded with challenges when first we step onto the transformational path – but as we embrace and learn from these, the road gets easier.

The true path is a long-term path, not one created from instant gratification. It unfolds before us in a divine order that we cannot foresee when first we step onto it. It is humble, based simply upon the guidance of our True Self, making no grand statements. This doesn't mean that what we create will be small or inconsequential however. On the true path, there is no need to rebel against the mass-consciousness. Instead, we become like a river flowing quietly. There is no need to tell others what to do. We simply live our truth and follow our bliss, and by doing this we become way-showers. Those who are seeking the same will identify with us and want to commune with us and our way of being, and those who do not, will move out of our sphere.

## The paradox

Change is inevitable, whether we choose it or not. If we deny change, we will still have to face it; if we align ourselves with it, we can embrace and enjoy the process of change.

## To become aware of

Here are some questions to ask yourself:

- If I could live my ideal life, what would it look like?
- What is stopping me from having it?
- Where do I feel stuck?
- What would it take to move out of this stuck-ness?
- What do I have to believe to remain stuck?
- What is the worst that could happen?
- What are my fears?
- What is the first step towards making a positive change in my life?

Positive change must start with you!

**Affirmations**

It is safe to listen to the inner guidance of my True Self.

Change is inevitable, and so I choose to embrace it.

I acknowledge and accept any fear of change.

Even though I have fears, I can choose change.

I now no longer allow fear to rule my life.

I now choose growth and transformation over safety and security.

I am willing to change for my highest good.

I choose to be courageous.

The Universe is on my side and forever propelling me towards my highest good.

Change is a process and I make changes one step at a time.

It is safe to choose new behaviours that are in my highest good.

It is safe to go beyond my comfort level.

It is safe to let go of all that is no longer serving me.

When I let go of the old, I create a space for the new.

My future has infinite potential.

I go with the flow of change.

Even though there is uncertainty, I choose to have faith and trust in the process.

Where there is uncertainty, there is a field of infinite possibilities.

I trust in the Universe to create my life anew.

# LIE NUMBER SEVEN

## LIFE IS A BATTLE

**The Truth:**

**Life is a dance!**

***The Universe is on your side, so surrender, trust and be joyful. When your essence is at ease, your life flows with ease.***

For many of us, life can feel like an uphill climb. Like warriors, we battle our way through life, with beliefs like:

- Life's hard
- I have to work hard for a living
- I've got so much to do
- I never get to do what I want
- I have to be successful
- You've got to fight for what you want

- I've got to get ahead.

As long as there is an enemy within – the ego mind - we will continue to view the outside world as our enemy, and manifest enemies, whether it be other people, stressful situations, or an overwhelming schedule. The more at ease we choose to feel, no matter what challenges we face, the more peaceful and smooth our journey becomes.

Through the old beliefs, we have created a world that focuses predominantly on outcomes, achievement, organisation, power, control, competition, efficiency and material wealth. Our modern world is the creation of the ego mind's belief that the world out there is not friendly, and we must fight or struggle for what we want. Striving to live up to the world's expectations of success, we believe that this will bring us happiness, and so we feel the need to push, force, control or manipulate to have what we want. Yet our belief in struggle only creates further struggle and overwhelm. We may achieve our goal, but peace and happiness will evade us. We will find that the more we push, the more resistance we come up against. Most of us are working within a framework that makes no allowances for what our True Self desires. Like sheep, we buy into an elusive dream, working hard, and feeling stressed more often than we feel happy.

## Surrender

The Source does not want us to battle and struggle through life. It wants to take care of us, and we can do this by surrendering to it. Surrendering is letting go and refusing to engage in struggle. It is the opposite of battling, and although it initially takes faith and courage, the reward is inner peace. When we surrender, we are saying to the Universe "I trust you to support me and take me to where I need to go, because I know you are working with me". If we have a desired goal, we trust that the Universe will co-create it with us, and if it doesn't, we trust that the Universe has something else planned for us which is in our highest good. If what we desire is in alignment with our True Self, the Universe will orchestrate for us all manner of happenings that our ego mind could never imagine or foresee. As human beings we are here to create and to expand to our full potential. If we don't have intentions or plans, we can surrender each day, trusting that the Universe will show us where we need to go and what we need to do.

***"When you get rid of your fear of failure, your tensions about succeeding … you can be yourself. Relaxed. You'll no longer be driving with your brakes on."***

***– Anthony de Mello***

## Creativity Vs Achievement

We have forgotten that there is a natural Universal rhythm, and "a time for everything under heaven". No matter what we desire or work towards, life is a process. Every obstacle that we face in life is a necessary lesson to temper us and an essential step on the creative journey. If we haven't achieved our goal yet, then we are not ready for it. Other experiences and lessons are more important right now than the manifestation of that goal. If we no longer wish to battle through life, we must transform the old lies of the ego mind and listen to and act from our True Self. The ego mind thinks that the achievement of the outcome is the prize; the True Self knows that the lessons and growth on the journey are the prize, because they challenge us to evolve, and to be creative, and from this creativity, we become more than what we were before.

## The Universal Flow

The natural Universal rhythm is often referred to as the Universal Flow, and it is only from here that we are able to manifest. There is no battle or struggle in the Universal Flow. Think of water flowing in a river – finding its way with ease around rocks and crevices, diverting its path whenever necessary, and always in constant flow. Water doesn't flow up; it only flows down. This is the path of least resistance, where life flows with ease. This is how we are meant to live.

## Acceptance Vs Resistance

Because the ego mind has a constant agenda which is so often in opposition to the What Is, we create a war between our inner world and our outer world. This will be felt internally as stress, anxiety, frustration or anger and the feeling of wanting to be somewhere else or doing something else. Acceptance, on the other hand, is a very powerful vibration where we no longer need to resist anything, or feel the need to run from anything. Instead we meet every present moment with total acceptance. If we are struggling to accept something, we can accept that we are struggling to accept it! Often, the very switch from resistance to acceptance resolves the problem, because resistance IS the problem.

## Accepting our feelings

If we are experiencing "negative" feelings, our ego mind will chide us with the thought "I shouldn't feel this way". Yet the only way to transform our feelings is by accepting them. We cannot change what we don't accept. If we are feeling sad, lonely, angry, frustrated or discontent, we must accept that is how we feel and that there is nothing wrong in feeling this way. If we fully allow the feelings to be there without judgment, we allow a miracle to unfold. Eventually the feelings move through us and out of us. If we don't accept and allow our feelings, we will attempt to deny them and push them away, which only represses them, keeping them in our energy field, snowballing into stuck energy that re-creates situations that re-trigger those feelings. It is time to stop fearing our "negative" feelings and own them!

## Acceptance doesn't mean agreement

The ego mind gets very attached to its point of view. If someone says or believes something we don't agree with, we can follow our ego and go into battle with the person, or we can listen to our True Self and accept their point of view. Acceptance doesn't mean agreement. If another person states a point of view that we do not agree with, we can accept their point of view without agreeing with it. If someone chooses to criticise us, we can choose to resist the criticism and get defensive, or we can choose to accept the criticism, run it by our own inner guidance system, take from the criticism what is useful to us, and let go of the rest. If we fail to manifest a goal that we have worked towards, we can resist the outcome and feel frustrated and angry about it, or we can accept the outcome we received and attempt it again in a different way.

## Collaboration Vs Competition

Believing that there is never enough, the ego mind fights for its share, competing with others for what it wants. Sharing and helping are not in the ego mind's capacity. Driven by the emotions of envy and jealousy, it is unaware that these very emotions block happiness and create negative karma. The True Self is happy for others because it knows that there is enough for everybody. In fact, the True Self enjoys helping others achieve happiness and success. It knows that whatever we give away will return to us, and that long-term fulfilling outcomes are manifested only through the win/win paradigm, not from the win-lose paradigm which so often creates hollow outcomes and empty victories. When we collaborate with others, we each get what we want.

## Spaciousness Vs Busy-ness

Most of us fight time. As we discussed a little earlier, many of us have become accustomed to being busy and living at a stressful pace. If life quietens down we become frightened by the emptiness. To the ego mind, busy-ness feels far safer than freedom and space. It believes that if every moment is filled with something to do, people to see or places to go, then we are living a purposeful life, when this is not necessarily true. We use busy-ness to mask our feelings of emptiness and powerlessness that would arise if we give up being busy.

We fear being alone and quiet with nothing to do because we fear facing ourselves. This is why the Buddhists tell us that meditation is "true fearlessness". If we can truly face ourselves, we can face anything! Some of us have experienced times of emptiness when our ego mind has bombarded us with negative thoughts, feelings of loneliness, hopelessness, meaninglessness and other negative emotions. This is normal when we begin to face ourselves – all sorts of repressions will come up. "It is better to stay busy," says the ego mind, however it is only by facing these negative thoughts and emotions that we can see them for what they really are – just fearful ego mind thoughts and their resulting emotions which aren't real – and when we truly know this, we can render them powerless.

By creating empty moments and making friends with whatever comes up, we will find a spaciousness that heals us. All we need to do is sit and allow ourselves to relax, accepting that who we are in that very moment of doing nothing is a worthy and loving being. Self-compassion is of great importance if we choose to meditate or simply sit with ourselves. It is in this spaciousness that we can make contact with the present moment and observe the negative thought chatter of the ego mind. Allowing spaciousness into our lives is one of the greatest gifts we can give ourselves, because from this quiet spaciousness we begin to get clarity and perspective, and divine inspiration.

## Relationship battles

Relationships become a battle when we do not accept other people as they are. The ego mind thinks:

- This person needs to change
- Why can't this person see my point of view?
- How can this person think that way?

- Why can't this person do what I would like them to do?

- This person is so difficult!

As a consequence, we stop loving the other person because they are not being who we want them to be. When we accept others just as they are, and cease judgment, we find inner peace. From the vibration of love and acceptance, change is far more likely than from a vibration of resistance. Our relationship with that person will either transform or it won't. We must realise that if we want a relationship to transform, the only person we can work on changing is ourselves. The ego mind will say "why should I do all the work?" It is unaware that through acceptance, we will be positively transforming ourselves and that this will always be of benefit to us, as well as our relationships.

There are times when we are going to feel blamed, criticised and attacked by those we love or people we know or work with, and at these times it's a challenge not to react. It takes great awareness to create enough space between something that is said or done to us, and our reaction. But it is essential if we wish to transform our relationships, that we bring awareness to ourselves and our responses. Responding from a calm and thoughtful place, as opposed to the angry wounded child, we avoid the negative spiral of communication that will ensue – and instead open an avenue to understanding, resolution and healing.

***Oh Divine Master, grant that I may not so much seek to be consoled as to console; to be understood as to understand; to be loved as to love.***
***For it is in giving that we receive – it is in pardoning that we are pardoned."***
***– St. Francis of Assisi***

## Win/win relationships

For any relationship to flow, we must work within the paradigm of win/win. Our True Self wants an outcome for our highest good, and the highest good of all, while the ego mind wants an outcome for "me". If we are dealing with individuals who are still operating from the win/lose paradigm, we can be vulnerable to unconsciously falling into the same vibration. The challenge will be to remain present and aware, and maintain the intention of positive outcomes for everyone. We may find that there are some people with whom win/win communication is impossible, such as people who bully, want to control or manipulate. In these situations, it is wise to step away and accept with grace that there are some people and situations that we are not meant that we are not meant to be in relationship with.

## Trusting others

Some of us have had experiences that have led to the belief that:

- I can't trust other people
- People will betray me
- People are out to get me.

If we possess a general mistrust of others, we attract to us on a regular basis those very people who are untrustworthy! This reinforces the lie that we cannot trust others, and so we re-create these situations over and over again. When we wake up and become aware that these people have come into our life to reflect back to us the lie we hold within, we have the power to change the belief and our life. The more we focus on and talk about the bad intentions of others, the more we draw these people to us. To dispel the lie that people are untrustworthy, we must allow the space for the possibility of creating another reality. Every time we interact with a well-intentioned person, we must practise gratitude, and by doing this we magnify and affirm what we do want, thus allowing the Universe to send more well-intentioned people into our field. The more of these people we experience in our lives, the more love and gratitude we feel and from this we create a positive spiral of attraction. Our belief gradually changes to "perhaps there are some trustworthy people in the world", and then to "I know there are trustworthy people in the world". When we start believing that there are many helpful and trustworthy people in the world, we enter a new reality that is full of well-intentioned human beings.

## Discernment

Many of us grew up believing in the lie that it is bad to say "no" – we may feel guilty and believe that it is unkind, unloving or selfish to deny another. If we are saying yes to situations because we fear letting others down and we would really rather say no, then we are betraying ourselves. Whatever we say yes to (and this includes the things we do not say no to), the Universe will send us more of. In order to create harmony in our lives, we must learn to be discerning, and allow into our lives the people, things and situations that are in alignment with what we truly want. If we are allowing in unwanted situations or toxic people, the Universe sees this as something that we want and will send us more!

If we are doing work that we don't like but agree to do it, the Universe will send us more. If we are under-charging for our services, the Universe will send us more people who want to underpay us. Saying "no" gives a very clear message to the Universe not to send us more of whatever it is we do not want.

## When things don't go our way

We all have times when things don't go the way we would like – the computer breaks, a friend lets us down, we lose money on an investment, there's a traffic jam when we need to attend an important meeting – from small frustrations to huge disappointments, life has a way of showing us that it is the Source who is ultimately in charge and not us. And yet we are all creators too. If we have not created what we want, we must learn to surrender gracefully when things do not turn out the way we would like them to. While we may not know why things turn out the way they do, we can be sure of one thing: We are not meant to be granted that wish at this time!

The spiritual reasons are manifold - it may be that the more important lesson is learning to be patient or to go with the flow; it may be that we are overly-attached to our desire and so it eludes us and we must learn to detach; it may be that the Universe wants us to dig deeper into our creative powers or to test us to see just how much we want it and how committed we are to having it. It could also be that the Universe wants to steer us in a different direction entirely to that which we desire. All we can do at such times is surrender with grace, and accept what is happening, trusting that the Universe is always working in our highest good, and forever guiding us to where we need to go.

## Illness

Most of us think of illness as something we do not want. If we get ill, we resist the condition. We "hate" the illness and go into battle with it. We often hear of people "battling" cancer or "fighting" a disease, seeing it as something separate to themselves, when in fact it is something that their very own body created. By choosing to accept and love an illness, we are loving a part of ourselves, and we then work with it and not against it. While there are many causes of disease, negative emotions such as stress, anger, resentment, frustration and hatred are a contributor. If disease was created out of fear, it can only be healed through love. This starts with acceptance. If we are ill, we must give love to ourselves and our illness.

## Success and failure

"Success" is a word that many of us associate within a limited criteria such as achieving a goal in our career and/or creating material wealth. Or it may be having the "ideal family" and living in the "dream house". If we view ourselves and our lives through the ego mind, we may feel that we are not successful enough, with thoughts like "I should have achieved this by now" or "I should be wealthier by now". Even when we reach our success, the ego mind raises the bar, keeping us from feeling successful and satisfied.

It is easy to get caught up in the vibration of the mass-consciousness and compare ourselves to others. Through the ego mind, we have believed that we must live up to a certain standard dictated by the outside world, but success is a concept that must be manifested on the inside. If it is not, no amount of material wealth or status will ever satisfy us.

The earthly concept of success creates a polarisation - if we are not "successful", then we are "failures". Failure is simply a desired outcome that is not yet manifested, yet some of us use it as a label that we put on ourselves or others. No person can be entirely a "failure" or a "success" as we all succeed and fail in various ways throughout life. Someone may succeed at making a lot of money, but fail to achieve happy personal relationships. Another person may achieve personal happiness but fail to make a lot of money. These are simplified scenarios, but the point here is that there is no such thing as complete success as we would like to believe, or complete failure. Thinking in terms of success and failure is ego mind thinking that creates internal misery.

## True success

Most of us do not take the time to consider what "success" truly means to us personally. True success has nothing to do with the beliefs of the mass-consciousness. Like abundance, true success is personal and holistic. Rather than thinking in terms of material wealth, status and achievement, it is time to define for ourselves what our true version of success is. If the success you desire is based only on an outcome and not a process, you are being guided by the ego mind. If the success you want is based only on financial and material gain, the ego mind is at play. If success means external recognition and/or fame, you can be sure the ego mind is in charge. Even if or when you achieve all your ego's desires, the outcome will not bring you long term fulfilment. We each have within us an idea of what will make us truly happy. True personal success will include:

- Doing work that is purposeful and enjoyable
- A sense of meaning and making a positive difference
- Feeling appreciated and loved
- Abundance/financial freedom
- Good health and wellbeing
- Happy and fulfilling relationships
- Time to relax and allow space
- Whatever else truly matters to you!

**Detaching from ego success**

When we become overly attached to the idea of success, we will criticise ourselves if we are not succeeding, so our love for ourselves will be conditional. In order to feel successful in our lives, we must love and approve of ourselves whether or not we are achieving anything! We must learn to praise ourselves whenever we do achieve a goal, no matter how small, and we must practise self-love and gratitude irrespective of whether we achieve our desired outcomes or not. We must focus on the journey and praise ourselves for the work we are doing each day, loving ourselves unconditionally, irrespective of our desired outcomes. This, ironically, will draw to us our desired outcomes sooner than berating ourselves and battling to achieve them. Think of employers you have had in the past. It was far more pleasant and productive working for a kind and encouraging boss, than working for a critical demanding one. Start by being that kind and encouraging boss to yourself.

**Purpose Vs work**

Enjoying our work on a daily basis is key to being in the Universal flow. The new energies are pushing us all towards a more purposeful life, aligned to our unique skills and talents, and so evermore people are wanting to work at something they feel excited and passionate about. Feeling ambivalent about our daily work can create an internal battle and take us out of the Universal flow. Loving our daily work brings us joy and from this vibration follows wellness and abundance.

For too long, we have believed the lie that we cannot do what we love and earn a living, and so we have ignored our true gifts and repressed our potential, not trusting that doing something we love will reward us. We all have gifts and strengths. When we employ ourselves with these gifts and strengths, we feel a deep sense of fulfilment. Many of us were told that these gifts and strengths were not "work" and therefore we could not justify them as a career. If we aspired to do the thing we were passionate about, we may have been told we were dreamers, and to get a "real job". Our parents may have told us "This is life. Be realistic. You need to earn a living". This was the reality for most of our parents' generation and those before them.

Some people do not flourish in their career because they are not aligned to their chosen career path. The path was either chosen for them (parents, teachers and society) or they chose it themselves based on the messages they received from the mass-consciousness:

- I achieved high grades at school, so of course I should go into law or medicine

- I chose to do this because it's highly paid

- I can't do what I would really like to do because I won't make enough money

- What will others think of me if I choose to follow my passion?

- There aren't enough jobs in the field I would like to work in

- I can't believe people would pay me for working at my passion.

Believing the lies, we follow in the well-trodden footsteps of our ancestors and choose to do work that pays the bills but does not necessarily inspire us. Even if we make a lot of money and achieve status, there may still be a sense that we are not fulfilled. Some may sabotage their progress, because they don't have the passion to sustain their energy in that field of work.

When we get in touch with our life purpose and follow that path, our paradigm of "work" changes, because when we do what we love, we no longer think of it as "work", and life is no longer a battle. If we are loving our work, we are truly blessed because we are able to express ourselves and enjoy our day-to-day experience, creating abundance through doing something we love. Even if we do not earn a high income, the day-to-day satisfaction will far outweigh the lack of a big pay packet. That is not to say that we won't earn a good income doing what we love – the belief that we cannot make a good income out of doing what we love is another lie to be let go of!

## Finding your purpose

While some of us have a deep knowing of what our purpose is, some of us don't know – and this can create a sense of struggle. I have met with many people who say "I haven't found my purpose. How do I find it?" The answer I tell them is "You don't. Your purpose finds you." And it can find us at any stage in life. Everybody is different, but we all have one thing in common when we recognise our purpose - when we are doing what we love, we feel deeply engaged and joyful; so much so that we can lose all concept of time and space.

If you are unsure of what your purpose is, surrender this question to the Universe and allow time and space to explore the things that interest and excite you. Work at whatever gives you satisfaction right now, and practise gratitude for your current work and income. It is wise to choose a job that does not rob you of all your energy and time, as this will sabotage your ability to explore yourself and your interests. Know that your purpose will be revealed to you in divine and perfect timing. Rather than worrying about finding your purpose, choose to live each day *on purpose*!

***"Your purpose in life is to find your purpose and give your whole heart and soul to it"***
***– Gautama Buddha***

## Shifting to purpose

Perhaps you know what you would like to do, but don't think it is possible to make the change. Deciding to live our purpose requires a paradigm shift. We must no longer believe the ego mind's lie that says:

"I must work in this job so as to make enough money to live".

Instead, we must listen to our True Self and know:

"By choosing to follow my purpose, I trust in the Universe to provide for me".

If we are in a position that seems impossible to move out of, we must surrender our desire to the Source and trust that it will send us the means to make the shift when the time is right – which it will, because not only are we given inspiration from the Source; we are also sent the means through which to do it! Most of us don't believe this, and so it doesn't happen. We can help the process along by visualising regularly what it is we want until we are in the feeling place of it. We may have to rely on another form of income such as other employment when first we step on to our chosen path, but as we begin to see the manifestation of the Universe supporting us, we can start to let go of the old channels of income, and create our abundance entirely through our passion or from other new channels that open up for us.

If we have grown used to the comforts of a certain income and lifestyle, we may have to let those go for a time, and live in a more simple way. Many people find that when they begin to live their purpose, they no longer need the comforts and rewards they had grown used to in their old life. These old comforts and rewards were needed in the past to survive the pressure and pain of not living true to themselves.

The Universe wants us to live our passion and follow our bliss, and in return it will look after us.

***"Follow your bliss, and doors will open where once there were walls"***
***– Joseph Campbell***

## Aligned action Vs work

The ego mind thinks in terms of "work". The True Self thinks in terms of "creativity" and "action". In order to create what we want, we must act from our sense of inspiration and vision. We must stay aware that our actions are in alignment with what we want, by asking ourselves:

*"Am I moving towards what I want or away from what I want?"*

If your actions are moving away from what you want, you will feel a sense of conflict. Your actions are powerful statements to the Universe, so be sure that they are aligned with your dreams. The Universe responds best to inspired action - this contains the energy of joy, excitement and enthusiasm. It is in opposition to the energy of "work", which most of us associate with exchanging energy/labour for money and does not necessarily contain joy, excitement or enthusiasm.

## Prioritising

Some of us struggle because we are not giving priority to what we truly value – such as how we want to feel, our wellness, our close relationships and our creative pursuits. If we no longer wish to struggle, we need to prioritise the things we value. To reflect on this effectively, imagine, after you have died, looking down at all you have left behind. What would you have wanted to achieve? What difference would you have liked to make? From this perspective, become aware of what your true values are, and be sure to attend to these on a regular basis before anything else.

### A shift of pace

Many organisations work at a fast pace, and expect turnarounds from their employees in timing that is not always conducive to human wellness, putting at risk the health and wellbeing of their employees. Some self-employed individuals also choose to work this way, driving themselves at a pace that is ultimately exhausting and damaging to their health and personal relationships. This is based on the ego mind's drive for efficiency and "more", and leads to imbalance, stress and illness.

The True Self knows that we are not meant to work at "God's pace". At this pace there is no struggle or stress. There is breathing time, time to think and contemplate, and time to relate to others with love. Think of the steady rhythm of the heart or the ocean tide. What we cannot do today, we continue tomorrow, in a balanced and fresh way. Ironically, when we choose this pace, we actually work more efficiently and creatively, and create more fulfilling outcomes. The more we allow ourselves to work at this pace, the more productive we become because we are operating from the peaceful vibration of love, not the anxious vibration of fear, which drains our energy and blocks creativity.

If we are employees, we must no longer allow the pressure from others and the stress of our work to sabotage our health and wellbeing. Unless we insist on a change with our employers, the same expectations will remain. These old structures cannot transform unless we do something about them. We must lose the fear that we will not be provided for if we walked away from a stressful job that is not good for us, and trust that when we act in our highest good, the Universe will provide an alternative for us. Many employees feel unable to speak out, in fear of losing their jobs, and yet loss of health and key relationships is a far greater price to pay in the long-run.

Some organisations are beginning to make positive changes in the way they treat their employees, creating from a win/win paradigm. Having happy and healthy employees creates a synergy whereby both employer and employee are rewarded in a holistic way.

The old "pressure" paradigm came from the age of productivity, where the harder we worked, the more we achieved or produced, and therefore the more profit. This age has been and gone. We are now in the age of creativity and this requires a paradigm shift that allows periods of spaciousness, so that our minds can open up and realise their full creative potential, no matter what work we do.

## Synchronicity manifests when we trust

When we are on our true path, we surrender to the Universal Flow and synchronicity happens in amazing, and very often surprising ways. This is the Universe orchestrating things for us - chance meetings, opportunities, fortuitous coincidences, helpful people and "strokes of good luck" begin to appear in our lives.

In the old paradigm, we were "battlers", working hard, feeling unsupported and alone, thinking we had to do it all ourselves. When we come to know that we are never alone, but always supported in a far greater way than we could ever imagine, we become co-creators. The celestial support is far greater than any human support, but we will only ever receive that support when we create time and space to know it and trust in it.

When we trust, we feel at ease and whatever we undertake is done in the vibration of inner-peace and love. We can tell ourselves that we trust in the Universe, but if we are feeling fearful and anxious, then we are not trusting. Thoughts that feed fear and anxiety will be based on a lie. We must stay aware of our thoughts and learn to identify and weed out the lies. Learning to trust is a process. We begin by paying attention to and giving thanks for every positive outcome, fortuitous event, helpful person or situation, because these are evidence that we are being supported and looked after. Keeping a journal of all positive happenings and reading back through it whenever we feel the vibration of fear creep in is a powerful way of keeping faith.

## Beauty

Beauty heals us, but many of us cannot see it because we are too caught up in our day-to-day struggle. Whether it be walking or sitting in a garden, watching a butterfly, seeing a sunset, admiring a painting, listening to music or taking the time to beautify our home, beauty is all around us. To see and feel beauty, we must slow down and become present. The more we are willing and open to see beauty and give thanks for it, the more beauty will appear in our lives. We begin to realise that each and every moment is sacred and we can see beauty even in the most mundane things - our daily tasks will be transformed into rituals to be enjoyed by bringing presence and love into them. Even tasks we do not like can become transformed if we allow. There is beauty in washing the dishes, doing the laundry, preparing our tax return or paying our bills!

For some, life can become small and mundane. Periods of illness, a disability or old age will often push us to transform and see our world from a different perspective. If we choose to see it, beauty can be sourced in any circumstance.

## 7 Daily Principles

Even if we have an inspiring vision for our lives, we must balance this with living on a daily basis. Here are seven daily principles with which to live your life:

**Live true to self**– listening to your own inner guidance, and not allowing others' values and expectations to influence you, unless they are in your highest good.

**Live in peace** – finding inner peace through meditation, being in nature, holding healthy boundaries with others and not identifying with outside drama.

**Live honestly** – being honest in your dealings with others and also with yourself.

**Live on purpose** – choosing words and actions that are in alignment with your values.

**Live in presence** – being conscious of being here in the present moment and not dwelling on the past or worrying about the future.

**Live in acceptance** – accepting every moment as if you have chosen it, allowing you to work with the moment and not against it.

**Live in gratitude** – focusing on what you do have, and consciously giving gratitude to the Universe for it.

## Life really is a dance, not a battle

When we no longer choose to battle through life, but surrender to presence and to love, we will create for ourselves a shift to bliss. The more we trust in the Universe, the more inner peace we will find within us, and this will be reflected back to us in our lives. Our lives will still inevitably contain the light and the dark – creativity, gains and joy as well as challenges, losses and sadness - but these will no longer have such a hold on us. We cannot have the light without the dark. We come to know that life is a cycle of experiences that come and go, building up and breaking down, forever changing, and we do not need to over-identify with any of it. If we have a bad day, we know that "this too shall pass" and if we have a wonderful day, we give gratitude and also know that it too shall pass!

## The Paradox

When we surrender, trust and allow our life to unfold to the will of the Universe, while at the same time holding the intention of what we truly want, we join in the Universal flow and allow outcomes for our highest good and the highest good of all.

## To become aware of

Stay aware of your vibration by checking in with your physical being. Feel your body and sense any need to not be in this present moment. Sense any need to push, force, control or manipulate. Sense any resistance, defensiveness, frustration or anger. Acknowledge these feelings. Then surrender to the What Is. Consciously breathe out and surrender your emotions and concerns to the Universe. Remind yourself that you are exactly where you are meant to be right here, right now. Imagine yourself to be a flowing stream of water. Choose to accept, in this moment, the circumstances of your life, just the way they are. Thank the Universe for divine resolution, and trust that events will unfold exactly as they are meant to. If you have a dream or a vision, surrender it to the Universe, and trust that if it is in your highest good, it will eventuate, and if it is not, something just as wonderful or even better will manifest!

**Affirmations**

I now surrender to the Universal Flow.

I give up the need to live in "overwhelm".

I surrender my desires to the Universe and I accept my life right now, just the way it is.

I accept every present moment just the way it is.

I trust in the Universe completely.

Life's lessons and growth are more important than any outcome.

I enjoy the journey and surrender the outcome.

I accept others just the way they are.

I accept others' points of view even if I don't agree with them.

I accept all my feelings.

I accept that the only person I can change is myself.

I now no longer need to compete with others; instead I collaborate.

I choose to operate from the paradigm of win/win.

Whatever I give away I get to keep.

I create True success from my True Self.

I let go of all self-judgment around failure.

Failure is what everyone experiences on the way to success.

I now give up the need to be busy, and I allow in spaciousness.

I am discerning about who and what I allow into my life.

It is ok to say "no".

I gracefully accept the What Is when things don't go my way.

I am well-intentioned and therefore trustworthy.

I attract to me well-intentioned and trustworthy people.

Today I choose to live my life on purpose.

I choose aligned and inspired actions towards my dreams.

I give priority to my highest values and give time and attention to what is important to me.

I choose to live and work at the Universal pace.

I surrender to the Universe and trust in its orchestrations and synchronicities.

I am open each day to seeing the evidence that the Universe is supporting me and give thanks.

Today I choose to feel trust.

Today I choose to see beauty.

I have a beautiful life and I am so grateful.

Thank You.

# IN CONCLUSION

## A SHIFT TO BLISS FOR THE WORLD

Most of us are concerned for the state of the world, and yet on the spiritual level, all is well. Within our societies, there are the "haves" and "have nots". The Western World countries have "too much" (in general) while other countries have "too little". Wars and the reign of terror have created fear, and there is a refugee/immigration crisis greater than ever before. There are ripples of fear throughout the world, as we fear the changes that are happening.

Where there is fear, love cannot exist. Fear blocks our empathy and compassion. Only love can heal our world. In any given moment, we have a choice as to whether we choose the vibration of fear or love. The populations of the world are blending like never before and while it may feel chaotic, this merging and cohabitation of religions and races is the beginning of a shift towards a more integrated human race.

In our vibration of scarcity and greed, a large proportion of the earth's inhabitants have not respected the Earth. We pillage its resources, with no thought to the balance of nature. Forests are disappearing and people and wildlife are losing their habitats. Most of us feel helpless, but the greatest way that we can each help the Earth is by waking up and to no longer live in fear. Living and creating from the vibration of love, we not only heal ourselves; we heal the world. Love is what the Earth needs. The Universe is holographic – not only are we a part of the Universe; the Universe is a part of us. When we lovingly create our own world of bliss from within our True Selves, we contribute to changing the Earth vibration to love.

It is futile to attempt to heal the world if we have not healed ourselves first. This we have attempted to do and inevitably failed, because the actions have not come from the vibration of love. Action aligned with love and truth will create positive outcomes. Giving to charities to help the starving will not solve the problem if we have not addressed and healed our own greed, because we are giving out of guilt and not transforming the vibration that created poverty or famine in the first place. Healing our greed and living balanced lives is the first step in creating a positive shift.

Attempting to save rainforests is pointless, unless we have an inner paradigm shift in how we see and use the earth's resources in our own lives. We must heal our fear of not having enough and operate from the paradigm of win/win. Equality for every human being will come about when we each realise that "more" doesn't mean "better", and when each of us knows that we are powerful beings who are capable of creating a wonderful life for ourselves, no matter what our circumstances are.

On the spiritual level we are all equal and not one person in this world is a victim. We are each here to realise this through the soul challenges we came here to transcend. Praying for world peace is futile if we are at war with ourselves, our families or our neighbours. Peace must begin within us. Every positive change we make for ourselves is a miracle that has a flow-on effect. As each of us, one by one, saves ourselves, we save the world.

# ABOUT THE AUTHOR

Nicole Bayliss is a Holistic Life Coach and Energy Healer who practises in Sydney, Australia. Her work focuses on assisting people through transformation and creating the lives they want. To subscribe to Nicole's mailing list or to contact Nicole, visit her website www.nicolebayliss.com.au.